From a Distance

Scattered Memories and Stories of Love

Kathy Billings

From a Distance: Scattered Memories and Stories of Love
Copyright © 2018 Kathy Billings
ISBN: 978-1-63381-153-9

Designed and produced by:
Maine Authors Publishing
12 High Street
Thomaston, Maine
www.maineauthorspublishing.com

Printed in the United States of America

Dedicated to my mother, my best friend,
who I talked to every day
whether or not she understood what I was saying—
although I bet she always did.
And, to my father,
who I thank profusely for his total trust in me.

PROLOGUE

I never got closer than a mile away, but every day my gaze was uncontrollably drawn in its direction. Every time I looked its way, a subtle curiosity enveloped my thoughts for a brief moment. There was a story to be told about this house, this home, about the lives within and around it. It became my obsession, and then my therapy, to tell this story because my mother couldn't.

~~~~~~~~~~~

It bewildered the residents of a small New England beach community—the untimely disappearance of the fifteen-year-old daughter of a local farmer during the peak of the summer of 1932.

It took the occasional foggy memory of a 91-year-old in the nursing facility of a nearby retirement community eighty-five years later to reveal fleeting glimpses of her past that would shed light on this heartwarming mystery. And, from a distance, her daughter listened to and untangled the interlocking stories of lifetimes not to be forgotten.

July 2016

*H*er stare is deep, leading me somewhere unknown.

"What do you remember about your first visit here in Maine?" I ask, hopeful that there will be a response. "Didn't you come here on vacation once as a child?" I have vague memories of hearing a story about this years ago, but my mother's childhood never interested me very much, certainly not in the way it does now.

"My birthday party," she answers with a slight glimmer in her tired eyes. She is not looking at me but out the window. Treetops with summer leaves flutter in the light offshore breeze. Billowing clouds dance above with a touch of blue in the sky. You cannot see the ocean. You cannot hear the ocean. But it is there—beyond the pine forest, below the rock ledge, off to the east no more than a quarter of a mile away.

My mother's home is now here—a small, sterile room down on the left of the Higgins Beach hallway in the nursing-center wing of this coastal Maine retirement community. The walls of her room are bare except for a white board with daily reminders of the month and day of the week. Occasionally, someone will draw a picture of a flower or a smiley face, or add the date of her next haircut appointment. A single window faces west; a few family photos are placed on surfaces around the room. A television is mounted in the corner, but she prefers the quiet. Her door to the hall is always open, and I make sure to open the window regularly to let in some fresh air. There are two chairs for visitors; she remains in bed unless transferred by the nurses to her wheelchair to go to meals. For some reason of which I will never be sure, she can no longer walk. Yes, she has been diagnosed with "moderate frontotemporal dementia," so I can only guess that is to blame for her immobility. It is hard to believe this is the same person who climbed the Himalayas at the age of 67 and who, until just recently, was enthusiastically walking her dog (the last of ten in her adult life) two or three times a day.

"Do you remember how old you were?" I continue, hopeful that I can tap the recesses of her long-term memory.

"No, but my sister was there. Your dad may remember."

Yes, I ponder, Dad may—he's always been good with dates.

Born in 1925, my mother was the younger of two daughters born to William and Marie, whose marriage did not last. The girls were raised in New York City by their mother but benefited from spontaneous showers of adventure and intrigue by their father. Their trip to Maine in 1932 (yes, Dad did remember the date, and a bit more) was one of those. A new inn had opened on the shores of the Atlantic at Higgins Beach in Scarborough, Maine. William, more commonly known as Bill ("Pa" to his girls), was always one to grasp at the opportunity to steal his daughters away to explore something new.

"What did you, Janey, and Bill do while you were on vacation? You were at the beach, right? You've always loved the beach; it must have been fun for you. How long did you stay? You had a birthday party. It must have been your seventh birthday. What did you do?"

So many questions. I wait patiently only to find her drifting off, losing focus. So few answers. Well, there's always tomorrow. I do visit almost every day, as something tugs at me when my feet first hit the floor each morning. I have the time now. I retired early from my career and recently bought a house nearby so that I can be close to her. I love her.

FRIDAY, JULY 15, 1932

*A*nnie woke to the early morning sun beating down on her face and her first smells of the ocean. At first she was confused, but when she glanced over at the bed next to her, she saw her sister deeply asleep under a simple but beautiful white coverlet just like her own. The dark wood walls of the almost perfectly square room were broken up by four windows and a door to the hallway. A salty, musty smell filled the air—the damp sea air working its way across the unpainted surfaces of the room. The ceiling was high with one small light, and a long pull string hung down between the two beds. In addition to the beds, a simple dresser and mirror graced one wall and a floor-length curtain concealed a small closet area. Annie smiled as she took in the cozy perfection of her temporary home away from home and recalled the excitement of her late arrival at this beach-side inn the night before.

An adventurous soul—unlike her rather moody older sister, who was quickly blossoming into a teenager and spent most of her time listening to the radio, eating, napping, and fussing in front of the mirror—Annie couldn't wait to take on the day and explore her new surroundings. Two whole weeks away from the strict routines of her city life—daily chores, rigorously scheduled meals, predetermined outfits coordinated with her sister's to suit the Upper East Side lifestyle her mother so naturally embraced. No, here at the beach, far from the crowded, bustling streets of the city and the forever watchful eye of her mother, Annie awoke to the anticipation of a world awaiting discovery. A world of sand, surf, sunshine, and, if she had it her way, adventure.

In the adjoining room on the second floor of The Breakers, Annie's father, Bill, rose and peered out the window to assure himself that the brand-new green Packard Roadster remained safely parked street-side where he had left it the night before. Now 36 years old, he had served as a combat pilot (first lieutenant) in France during the era of the "flying crate" planes in World War I. After the war, he'd spent two years as an advertising executive for the Packard Motor Company, and to this day, he was privileged to borrow one of their latest models whenever he wanted. This trip to Maine with his almost seven- and twelve-year-old daughters was the perfect opportunity to ride in the style of the day.

Despite the fact that the Dow Jones industrial average had just hit its lowest point of the Great Depression (bottoming out at 41.22 just one week before), Bill's conservative Yankee habits had kept his "vacation stash" safely protected. Now he had two whole weeks alone with his girls, whom he hadn't seen since Christmas, seven months before.

"Hey, you two!" he called as he came through the door, and two curly-haired heads popped out from beneath the billowy white covers. "Time to rise and shine—lots to explore!"

Immediately jumping from her bed, Annie ran to the window to get her first glimpse of what would soon open the door to a new chapter in her life. In awe, she looked up at her father standing next to her. His eyes twinkled and his soft mustache formed a bridge between the unforgettable creases created by his generous smile. He was a handsome man who emitted warmth and tenderness to those he loved.

"Pa! Look how far away the ocean is!" Annie exclaimed. "I thought the waves were hitting the rock wall by the road when we got here last night."

"It's the tide, dearie," Bill explained. "Every six hours it goes from high to low and then back again—a change of about nine feet each time. A nine-foot tide can mean changes of up to seventy-five feet in the amount of beach there is between us and the waves. Right now, it looks to be what they call 'dead low tide.' It's a wonderful time to walk on the beach and explore all its wonders."

"Then let's go!" Annie hollered as she rushed to the carpet bag full of beachwear, knickers, shoes, and caps. No frills for this trip, just the most ragged, comfortable clothes a budding tomboy could ever ask for.

"Wake up, Janey!" she screamed at her sister. "Pa says it's time to explore the beach!"

Holding back laughter, Bill quietly left the girls to work out their morning routine while he shaved and dressed in his room. His marriage had only lasted thirteen years, but now he had two precious daughters with unfaltering love and trust in him.

After a quick breakfast on the open porch while watching and listening to the distant waves and seagull cries, the beach blankets were gathered and the three set off to discover their new surroundings. It was early yet, just 7:15 a.m., so they claimed the beach, Higgins Beach, as their own. The nighttime tide had left piles of seaweed scattered about spewing tiny secrets of the sea—baby crabs, periwinkles, mussel and clam shells, pebbles of all sizes and colors. In the newly cleansed sand, a close eye might also come upon pieces of sand dollars (or, with luck, a whole one) and the curving paths of snails feeding just below the surface. Facing the sea, off to their right were rocky ledges and tidal pools that would distract them for hours; to the left, a half mile of flat, sandy beach reached out into a rippled point extending into the ocean and welcoming them to the mouth of the Spurwink River.

It was well after noon when the rising tide guided them back to the immediate shore, where a small group of sunbathers had set up their blankets, umbrellas, and picnics—mostly families with small children and young couples enjoying the midday sun. Bill and Janey headed back to the inn to wash up for lunch. Turning to look back at the beach, Annie quickly excused herself and headed right back to the sandy shore.

"Can't control that one," Bill chuckled as he and Janey headed inside. "She'll be back when she realizes how hungry she is!"

A wagon, a man, a girl, a dog. That's what had pulled Annie back to the beach. Her curiosity guided her toward a farmer and his daughter collecting seaweed. Working with long iron rakes, they hurled the slimy, black and green vegetation left in piles by the tidal currents into their wagon. Without hesitation, Annie grabbed a pile of the seaweed in her arms and hoisted it into the wagon. The girl, probably not much older than Janey, smiled at Annie and the dog barked his approval. Annie smiled and waved as she turned and quickly ran back to the inn.

August 2016

"*P*a!" erupts from her mouth as her eyes open wide, suddenly, catching my attention.

"What, Mom?" I ask, realizing that I must grasp this rare moment of wakefulness. "Yes, Dad told me that your Pa took you and Janey to the beach here in Maine for a vacation in 1932—you were turning seven and it was after your year in Switzerland." (During their parents' divorce in 1931, my mother and her sister had been sent to a private school in Switzerland, but my mother's memories of this seem to have faded long ago.)

"I made a new friend at the beach. We played and I helped her collect…"

"Collect what, Mom?"

A long pause. I wonder what she might be struggling to bring to the surface of her fragile mind.

"It smelled and…there was a wagon. My friend had a dog."

6

A new friend. A dog. A wagon. Something smelly they collected on the beach. No mention of sunbathing, swimming, gathering shells. As her words turn to mumbles, her eyes close, and, once again, she drifts away. She is relaxed, comfortable, curled on her side hugging the stuffed puppy my sister gave her, seemingly at peace, which is all I really hope for these days. Piecing her words together, the image of a spirited outgoing tomboy—the child I always imagined my mother to be—is, if only slightly, confirmed.

I sit, welcoming the stillness that follows as I watch my mother's chest rise and fall, and then I close my eyes to join her in the calming essence of the moment. I have come to look forward to sharing this space with her, to joining her in this odd sense of tranquility so uncommon to both of our "normal" lives.

I look up at the institutional, plastic, black and white, round wall clock in her room—11:20 a.m.—time for the thirty or so residents to gather for lunch in the dining room at the end of the hall. The nurses arrive to transfer Mom to her wheelchair—the only time I witness her anxiety, but it passes quickly and we venture out into "the world." Eight round tables crowd the narrow dining space, generally four to a table, most of who are in wheelchairs. (I never realized how many different sizes, shapes, and configurations of wheelchairs existed!) Some residents are accompanied by nurses or caregivers to assist them with eating. A few are managing the task even though they appear to be sound asleep. Staff place bowls of soup, rolls, and drinks, most covered in plastic wrap and labeled with names. (Mom's name is always spelled wrong: Anne. Sorry; no *e*!)

Mom and I join her regular table of four, which includes Mary, Phyllis, and Anna, with smiles and greetings that last but a few seconds. Although conversation is lacking, to say the least, I sense that true affection for each other is not. Slight Mary, the most talkative, shares stories of her black lab, her time living in

Europe, and her special dietary preferences (the asparagus always ends up in a pile on her napkin and she rarely eats meat). Anna says little but makes it clear that she is unhappy with the meal and the service. Phyllis, my favorite in the group, sits directly across from me and Mom, raising her head slightly every so often with the warmest smile I have ever seen. Very small in stature and always well groomed, Phyllis wears lovely sweaters and finely appointed jewelry, each hair falls gently in place, and she emits a charm and grace, embedded in total silence, that conveys a deeper soul that I want to know.

One day last week, Phyllis's daughter had joined her for lunch, and I was able to discover that Phyllis had grown up locally. Not wanting to pry, I learned little more. (I try always to respect the privacy earned at the end of one's life.) Phyllis does seem intent on my conversations with Mom. I wonder what's behind those sweet smiles that catch me off guard as I attempt to provide some sense of normalcy in this unexpected world that I have joined my mother in. Dementia is a mysterious illness, at least to me. It seems to manifest itself in many forms, none of which is easily understood. Everyone here seems to have their own version of it—it seems to be the universal diagnosis of what to me is simply a reality of "getting old."

Saturday, July 16, 1932

Thick fog engulfed the seaside, and the cool dampness forced Annie to throw off her covers and get up to close the windows before dashing back to the warmth of her bed. It was early yet, and the activities of the day before begged for some reflection as she waited for sounds of life in the inn.

After their morning exploring the beach from one end to the other and discovering treasures in the simplest of places, Bill, Janey, and Annie had enjoyed a lunch of fish chowder and oyster crackers at the Silver Sands, a slightly larger beach-side inn a few cottages away from The Breakers. Naps followed and then a walk up to the general store, The Pavilion, for an afternoon treat: fresh local ice cream blended with wild Maine blueberries in a thick, creamy float! The store and the narrow dirt streets that formed a grid of small shingled cottages were bustling on that summer Friday afternoon as families and businessmen arrived from the nearby cities of Portland and Lewiston-Auburn for their weekend getaways, and tourists burdened with bags and trunks welcomed the beginning of their summer vacation. Most had arrived by carriage from the town's trolley stop a few miles away. Others had come in their personal cars, the Ford Model A being the most popular.

Bill, Janey, and Annie had perched on barrels outside the store, taking in the sights and sounds of this tiny yet thriving summer community. Curiosity took Annie's attention away as she caught a glimpse of a wagon cresting the hill and coming into view from the beach. Overflowing with seaweed, the wagon passed by close enough for Annie to recognize the girl and the dog. A full load—a day's job done—heading home. Annie waved hopefully and received a smile of acknowledgment as the wagon pulled away. Her first day had seemed to open up a world of possibilities that bubbled within her as Annie returned to the inn with her father and sister for dinner and a game of cards—a proper and comfortably casual evening.

This Saturday morning, gazing out the window for a second time, the beach seemed a totally different place, the fog so thick that only the rocks and sand butting up to the immediate shore were visible. What on earth would keep her entertained on such a gloomy day, Annie wondered. Still early, the sun barely casting its rays through the gray mist outside, Annie crept quietly out of the room and descended the stairway in hopes that it was not too early for something to eat.

The inn was small—only eight guest rooms: four on the second floor and four on the third. Guests shared two bathrooms complete with all the modern conveniences of the day. Indoor plumbing was one of the newly opened inn's marketing features. On each floor, two of the rooms faced the sea, including one on the third floor in the inn's distinctive tower, while the other two faced west overlooking the street lined with well-kept summer cottages and gardens. Annie would soon discover that each cottage had a name—Beach Rose, Spurwink, Bird's Nest, Water Song, Sand Dune, and so on—given, in part, to guide the mail carrier, as no street numbers were assigned to the houses. The first floor of the inn held the office, a small library with a large central fireplace, the dining area and adjacent kitchen, and access to the open beach-side porch lined with wicker rocking chairs and pots of geraniums. This morning, as Annie descended the stairs, she found the dining room bustling and every table occupied. Aromas of bacon and coffee greeted her as she peered around hoping to find an empty seat.

"Care to join me?" a soft male voice summoned from a table for two by the window.

Not sure if it was appropriate to respond to, much less accept, the offer of a perfect stranger, particularly a man, Annie stood speechless and hoped her father and sister would appear. The gentleman rose and approached her with a gentle smile and a welcoming hand.

"Uh, I really should—" Annie started to reply shyly.

"But please do," the man, quite young and casually dressed, continued. "It appears that this is the only empty seat at the moment, and I'd enjoy the company."

Allowing a little chuckle to emerge, Annie quickly disregarded the teachings of her city upbringing and took the seat across the small table.

Jim was his name, and conversation came easily for both. Annie told him of her arrival the day before for a two-week vacation with her father and sister, a welcome escape from the city routine she abhorred. She could not hide her eagerness to explore every part of her new surroundings. Listening attentively, Jim smiled kindly, imagining himself at her age, when he had been fortunate to spend every summer here at Higgins Beach.

Jim was raised in an upper-middle-class family from Portland, the largest city in Maine and just five miles north. His father had worked most of his career for a local bank, but had recently moved with Jim's mother and sister to Michigan seeking a more lucrative job in the automobile industry as the Great Depression fell upon the country. At the age of 22, Jim had declared his independence, stayed behind, and secured a job with the S.D. Warren Paper Company so he could continue to enjoy time at the beach.

In the early 1900s, close to the time of his birth in 1910, Jim's parents had built one of the original fifty or so Higgins Beach cottages as the little oceanside community blossomed on what had been a sprawling farm. Jim had grown up spending every summer here and was happy to satisfy Annie's growing curiosity about the area. He told her about beach picnics, complete with bonfires, that typically ended with a game of hide-and-seek in the neighbouring bathhouses after dark. He described scavenger hunts along the beach when he and his friends competed to find sand dollars, seagull feathers, pieces of lobster traps and other fishing gear, crab shells (only with all the legs attached!), periwinkles, and, if you were lucky, a penny. He spoke fondly of Al, a local lobsterman who worked offshore at the mouth of the Spurwink River to provide fresh lobsters not only for tourists and the Portland market, but also as a regular treat for the locals.

"I'll make sure that you meet Al while you're here," Jim noted as he looked out at the fog. "I'll see if he'll take you out in his dory so you can see the beach from the water. It's an amazing view—on a clear day, that is."

Jim and Annie finished their breakfasts just as Bill and Janey emerged from the living room, clearly relieved to find Annie but also showing a bit of concern about her company.

"Pa! Janey!" Annie exclaimed as she jumped from her seat toward them. "Come meet Jim—he really *lives* here!"

Holding back laughter, Jim stood and politely greeted Bill and Janey. "Hello, Mr. Walling. So nice to meet you. Your daughter has told me you're here for a bit of a vacation, and I've been letting her in on some of the local charm. I grew up here—and, oh, yes, my name is Jim Harding. It's very nice to meet you."

With a relaxed sigh, Bill accepted Jim's handshake (very mature for such a young man, he thought), commenting that today was certainly not much of a beach day.

"Fog," Jim pronounced noting Bill's despairing glance out the window. "Some here actually welcome the reprieve from the summer sun and heat. It offers up a chance to be creative with one's time."

Bill wasn't convinced that the fog would offer up much for him and his task of entertaining two young girls. With a deep sigh, he looked hopefully at Jim for some suggestions to spur his creativity.

"Have you ever visited Portland?" Jim inquired. "It's but a trolley ride away, and if you're so inclined, I plan to go this morning and would enjoy the company. I usually visit the municipal market on Saturdays—many of our local farmers sell their products there, and it's always a good way to catch up on the latest news. I also like to help out the innkeepers when I can, saving them a trip to buy produce for the coming days."

"You must be a regular here," Bill noted as Jim led them to a larger table, now empty, so that Bill and Janey could enjoy some breakfast of their own.

"Yes," Jim said. "Since the inn opened in May, I've come every weekend. Today I'm starting my summer vacation, so I'll be here for at least a week, if not two. You see, my parents used to own a cottage here—they sold it two years ago when they moved to Michigan—and I know the couple that just opened the inn. In fact, for the past few months, I've been helping them prepare for the big opening. In return, they've held the third-floor tower room for me for the entire season, a most generous way of saying thank you."

Considering Jim's offer of a trip to Portland, Bill looked to the girls for their reactions and saw huge smiles beaming on their faces. They arranged to meet Jim at the trolley stop in an hour.

SEPTEMBER 2016

*M*om is most alert at lunchtime, which is on the early side for me—11:30 a.m.—so my visits are scheduled accordingly. She has been here for fourteen months now, and I visit as much as possible. For the first nine months, my visits required a one-hour drive each way, but this past May, I moved and am now only five minutes away. Happily, I now spend some time with her almost daily. I have never felt closer to her.

After our lunch, I try to get her out for some fresh air. At first we managed fifteen- to twenty-minute walks, always with my dog in tow. I tried to find a mirror to mount on the arm of her wheelchair facing backward so she could see me as I pushed her. No luck. Although her eyesight is severely limited she always senses the ocean when we travel the circular path looking east over the vast, beautiful sea. I do know that at least she can hear and smell it and feel those undeniable, unforgettable sea breezes that graze her face. It is a scene she knows well: not too long ago it was normal for her to take her dog for an hour at a time down to neighboring Higgins Beach for daily walks. They were known by all who lived in the small cottages lining the streets she meandered through. She was never one to simply pass by someone in their yard, and rather lengthy, comfortable conversations made her a welcome visitor to the neighborhood.

Now on our short walks on the paved walkway, I often stop and sit on a bench so that we can face each other and talk. I speak slowly and clearly, watching to make sure she hears me.

"Tell me more about your vacation here at the beach when you turned seven." It's a suggestion I seem to make repeatedly. I have come to realize, however, that the best trait I can possess these days is *patience*. (I even tell my dog this when she looks at me with those big questioning eyes as we experience this new world together.)

"We had a fun day in the city…at a market. I saw my friend."

Her response excites me. "What was your friend's name?" I ask hopefully. I wait.

Nothing. We gaze over the evergreens and watch a seagull soaring majestically overhead. We listen to the sounds as small waves lap against the rock ledges below.

"That's enough," I hear as Mom makes it very clear that she is done for this day.

Making our way back to her building, I try to extend the walk by noting the flower beds we pass, the birds on the many feeders residents have put outside their doors, greeting the occasional passerby.

"Are you OK?" she asks me regularly. Despite all that she is experiencing—fading memory, inability to walk, lack of vision, even the weight of her own weakened body—she always wants to make sure that I am all right.

"I'm fine, Mom," I reassure her, holding back but one of so many tears I know will flow from me someday.

SATURDAY, JULY 16, 1932

*I*t turned out to be a day that Annie would never forget! Now back at The Breakers washing and dressing for dinner, she tried to decide what would live on in her memory about this second day of vacation.

It wasn't the trolley ride, the tours down the tree-lined streets of Portland looking up at the towering brick buildings. It wasn't the smell of the fish market and boats docked at the many piers along Commercial Street. It wasn't the constant honking of cars rushing up and down the intersecting grid of streets, the bantering of farmers as they pushed their carts to the market square, or the laughter of children chasing pigeons in the park. It was *her*—the girl from the beach the day before, the girl with the dog, the girl riding atop a pile of seaweed on a wagon driven by her father—the girl now here at the market collecting coins from eager customers.

Annie remembered watching her work beside her father at the market, loading baskets along the pathway with produce and bouquets of beautiful flowers for the passersby—working tirelessly as the wagon was quickly emptied of its contents. But most of all, she remembered the moment the girl turned to her with a welcoming smile and then turned, with an even broader grin and a bit of a blush, as she looked away from Annie to Jim.

"Dad? Can I take a few minutes?"

Annie turned as the girl hollered and she and Jim approached the wagon. Looking up wearily, the girl's father turned away as if he hadn't heard her.

"Dad!" she exclaimed again, trying to get his attention. "Jim's here with some friends. I'll be right back."

Jim. The girl couldn't remember when he had not been a part of her life. For all of her fifteen years, he had been there as a friend, a companion, a confidant, a big brother, and now, the secret love of her life. He was of average height, rather lean and well-tanned, sporting a head of dark curls over big brown eyes and a smile that reflected his soft, gentle soul. Dressed for the city, Jim looked handsome in his tailored gray slacks, collared white shirt, woolen vest, and pencil-thin tie.

"Hey, Peanut!" Jim greeted her enthusiastically. "Come meet the Wallings—Mr. Walling and his daughters, Janey and Annie. They're vacationing at The Breakers."

"Bill, please," Annie's father responded as he reached for Peanut's hand.

"This is their first trip to Maine," Jim continued. "They've come from New York for a two-week hiatus at our very own Higgins Beach. With the fog as it is today, I invited them to join me on my trip to the market. Mr. Walling, Annie, Janey—this is my friend Peanut. She lives with her father on a farm quite close to the beach, and they come to the market every Saturday to sell their goods."

"You sure look busy this morning," Jim noted, turning to Peanut. "Everything OK?" his eyes cautiously shifted toward her father.

"I'm fine," Peanut said reassuringly.

Annie sensed tension but was easily distracted by thoughts of the dog. "Where's your dog?" Annie asked with excitement.

"Oh, Hobbs. He's hiding from all the hustle and bustle, probably under the wagon. He may remember you from the beach yesterday—I do," Peanut said fondly just as the dog bounded out to greet Annie.

"Your name is Peanut?" Annie asked, looking back and forth between Peanut, Jim, and Hobbs. She patted the dog's head absently.

"Well, she is to me," Jim interjected. "It's a long story. We've known each other for a long time. Her father owns the farmland across the river from the beach with his brothers. It's been in the family forever. As you can see, he keeps himself very busy, and he never has much to say. He's always been the quiet type, especially ever since his wife, Peanut's mother, died unexpectedly four years ago."

Not sure how to respond, Annie looked around for her father and sister, but they had wandered off to visit the other farm stands. "I think I should catch up with Pa," she said as she gave Hobbs another pat. "You probably need to do your errands, Jim. I'll catch up with Janey and Pa. Should we just meet you back at the trolley?"

The next two hours flew by. Annie and Janey bounced from wagon to wagon amazed at the amount of fresh produce, fish, meats, breads, flowers, and handicrafts on display and passing rapidly from hand to hand as men, women, and children filled their baskets. Everyone seemed to be enjoying this Saturday morning ritual. In the meantime, Bill had crossed the street to admire the long row of parked roadsters in front of the municipal building. Nothing compared to his Packard, but inspecting these four-wheeled wonders kept him amused.

The blanket of fog had thinned but not lifted when the foursome arrived back at The Breakers. The midday sun struggled to break through—a beautiful display of light streaming down in thin rays barely touching the ground.

Not having eaten since breakfast, they ordered afternoon tea service, a nice mix of miniature sandwiches and sweets—a slight reminder of city life. The day was still young, at least for Jim, who offered to take them for a walking tour of the beach community.

"Enough walking for me for one day," sighed Bill. "I think I'll pass. Janey? Annie? You're free to join Jim if you want."

More inclined to retire with her summer reading, Janey excused herself while Annie, on the other hand, had no inclination to pass on the opportunity to explore some more.

"Actually, let's take the bikes," Jim suggested. "In fact, in the shed behind the inn is a bicycle built for two we could borrow. Have you ever ridden one, Annie?" No response. "No? Well, you're in for a treat."

And that she was! For the rest of the afternoon, Jim pedaled her up and down the dirt streets and paths, waving at the neighbors and laughing as Annie let out a scream at every turn. Occasionally, Jim had to fend off a barking dog or veer around beachgoers loaded down with baskets of blankets and beach toys, but after a good twenty minutes or so, they reached the north end of the community where the cottages ended and a bare stretch of beach spread out before them.

"I need a break," Jim sighed as he climbed off the bike and held it steady until Annie had safely dismounted.

"That was fun!" Annie said. "Nice to stop, though. My bum doesn't feel so good!"

Laughing as if they were old friends, Jim and Annie leaned the bike against the beach rose bushes at the side of the street and headed onto the beach. An afternoon sea breeze had picked up and pushed the fog bank off to the north. It was mid-tide, and the view took Annie's breath away. This was the widest section of beach, reaching out in a rippled pattern to the mouth of the Spurwink River. Beyond that, a neck of land reached into the sea, mostly fields of farmland separated by stands of tall pine trees.

"That's where Peanut lives," said Jim, pointing at the spit of land sticking out into the ocean just east of them. "Her family, the Jordans, own the whole point, and she and her father live in that house on the end, the one with the tower—a bit like the tower at the inn, don't you think? I'm not sure, but I've always thought these towers were built so people could look for ships offshore."

Annie peered across the water at the house as Jim continued.

"And can you see that tree, just to the left of the house? It looks kind of like an umbrella. It's been there forever. Peanut climbs it all the time."

"You said you've known Peanut a long time." Annie looked at Jim curiously as they settled upon some rocks that separated the beach from the dunes. "How *did* she get the name Peanut?"

Jim folded his hands in his lap and stared at the distant point. After a long pause, he began to tell his new friend the story of Peanut.

DECEMBER 2016

*W*e enjoy what would be Mom's last Thanksgiving together with us as a family. Dinner is in the main dining room, where light bouncing off the ocean graces the attractive east-facing third-floor gallery. The tables are set with white linen and china, full-service silverware, and delicate centerpieces. It looks beautiful—not at all what one would expect in a retirement community. We have chosen the first of three seatings, 11 a.m., to accommodate Mom's customary schedule. A buffet of shrimp cocktail greets us as we are escorted to our reserved table. I ask a waitress to take a picture of Mom and Dad seated at the table with me, my sister, and my brother standing behind. Everyone is smiling, and Mom looks wonderful in her red sweater and pearls. Another buffet awaits with salads, turkey with all the fixings, pies and cakes. We are treated by attentive wait staff. It is a happy, almost normal time.

With Christmas approaching, her second here in the nursing center, on my next visit I pull from her bureau drawer some decorations I had brought last year. A snow globe, a stocking, red and green tinsel, and a bundle of little red ribbons. She sleeps as I put things around. I don't know if she will ever notice my handiwork, but it does make me feel complete about marking the holiday season, if even in a simple, almost tacky way.

I water the amaryllis bulb I just brought in for her knowing that she *will* watch it grow and get some pleasure out of that.

"Bye, Mom." I kiss her forehead. "See you tomorrow."

SATURDAY, JULY 16, 1932

*J*im found it difficult to believe that he, at the age of 22, was about to confide in such a young girl from New York City whom he had just met. There was something about her, though, something so easy and comforting, and he certainly did need someone to talk to. There was also something about this place, this beach, that drew out his innermost feelings—the ones that resided uneasily in his heart and soul, eating away at his core. And deep down, he realized that Annie reminded him of his sister, the one he had lost so many years before.

Jim was in love with Peanut, and Peanut was in love with Jim. They had known each other their entire lives—or at least hers, she being only 15 to his 22—and their consensual romance was a secret that was becoming harder and harder to keep.

Peanut was an only child who had lost her mother when she was only 11. She had been very close to her mother, her father seemingly having chosen his pleasures elsewhere. He had always been a hardworking man, a farmer, a carpenter, a typical man-of-all-trades, and he had always provided for his wife and daughter. But he preferred to spend his leisure time, what he had of it, in places unknown to Peanut and her mother. And he had a temper.

Peanut had grown up on the far point of the peninsula just north and east of Higgins Beach. The entire point of land was owned by the multigenerational Jordan family. Peanut's father was one of four Jordan boys, somewhere in the middle of the mix and by far the most detached and independent of them all. His house was a simple two-story farmhouse to which he had added a three-story tower to provide himself with rooms away from the women and the confines of their domestic world. He always joined them for dinner but otherwise preferred the solitude and privacy of his tower. No one ever joined him there; in fact, the door from the main house was usually locked from the tower side, and he managed to keep this space and its use to himself.

After Peanut's mother died—the circumstances of which she was never told—her father vacated the tower, kept it fully under lock and key, and moved into the main house to oversee the comings and goings of his daughter. For Peanut, it was as if she now had two lives—one that had just ended, a life of regularity, comfort, warmth, and love—and another that had just begun, one of labor, harshness, the unknown, and even fear. Her father never hurt her, but he forced her into a lifestyle very unlike the one she had known when her mother was there. Basically, at age 11, her childhood was over.

Jim had met Peanut when she was just a little girl and he a teenager enjoying summers with his family at their Higgins Beach cottage and working at the Jordan horse farm, which was owned by one of Peanut's uncles. Jim mucked the stalls, piled bales of hay in the barn, groomed the horses, repaired fencing, and did whatever other chores needed tending to.

Peanut was a regular visitor at the horse farm, sneaking down the wooded path along the rocky shoreline from her house whenever she could break away from her own chores. She loved the horses, and her uncle kept her visits a secret. He was aware of her father's harsh treatment of her and did whatever he could to make sure she was happy and safe. She was always a welcome visitor, and Jim enjoyed her company as well.

At home with her mother, Peanut had helped with just about everything to keep the household running. Even at a very young age she had pitched in with the laundry, cleaning, cooking, and tended to the large vegetable garden and hen house. After her mother died, those tasks not only became more demanding, but her father also expected her to help with some of the more difficult chores. As if she were a boy, he taught her how to change a wheel on the wagon, repair a split-rail fence, clean and sharpen the tools, and, as if she had the time, help him rake seaweed on the beach that they used to fertilize the fields. It was hard work from sunrise to sunset, every day of the week except Sundays, but Peanut had no choice. The only blessings that graced her solitary, hardworking childhood were her dog and the times that she managed to slip away to visit her uncle, the horses—and Jim.

Raking seaweed was actually the one chore Peanut looked forward to. It was most lucrative in the month of July when rockweed, a type of seaweed, was washed ashore by the incoming tide and lay in piles along the beach as the tide receded. This natural fertilizer was in high demand by local farmers, and Peanut's father had laid claim (she knew not how) to Higgins Beach. During the month, Peanut and Hobbs eagerly accompanied her father, traveling by horse-drawn wagon off Jordan point, across the bridge spanning the Spurwink River, and down the main road to the left turn that brought them to the small summer community and the half-mile stretch of beach. Hobbs would announce their arrival, barking at the many children and their dogs playing along the way. As they approached the beach, a quick glance to the right always brought a big smile to Peanut's face as she spotted Jim standing on the porch of his family's cottage, waiting, waving.

"Is her name really Peanut?" Annie asked again, having never known anyone with such a weird name. "Does everyone call her that?"

"Well, yes…I guess so. At first, it was my special name for her, but it seems to have caught on. You see, when she first started helping her dad collect the rockweed—she must have been only four or five years old then—she thought she was collecting peanuts." Leaning forward, Jim reached for a sprig of the brown and green seaweed at their feet. "See how these bulbs look?" he pointed out. "Well, Peanut thought they were really peanuts; in fact, she was known to have tasted them —salty and crunchy, I hear! Want to try?"

Laughing together, Jim and Annie decided to discard the seaweed and head back for ice cream at The Pavilion.

MARCH 2017

December, January, February, March…a snowy winter passes. Trips with Mom, even for but a few breaths of fresh air just outside the door, become less frequent. It is too cold. The sun is too bright. I would have never in my life thought that Mom, of all people, would not embrace a sunny winter's day.

Her interest in meals also begins to wane. Even corn on the cob has lost its attraction. We switch her to soup in a mug and half a sandwich, most of which goes untouched. Coffee ice cream and a cookie remain the high point of the meal for her—actually, for both of us.

Phyllis is in Florida with her daughter for the winter. Mary is still with us and keeps the conversation going as best she can. The dining staff helps liven things up, and Mom welcomes the back rubs she always gets, along with big smiles, from Lisa, our favorite.

Equipped with local news items, a childhood story or two involving my mother, an update on Dad, my kids, or my siblings, I do my best to carry on some sort of normalcy during the hour-long lunchtime. Mom and I are often the last to leave the dining room, and she seems most comfortable during those few minutes that we have there together, alone. No words tend to pass between us; they don't need to. We both seem to know where we are, what is happening, and that all we can do is be most grateful for this precious time at each other's side.

Lunch is over, but today Mom doesn't seem quite ready to return to her room, which in reality means her bed. The hallways are limited, but we make the most of it, greeting other residents, nurses, visitors, commenting on the new babies in the fish tank or watching Doug doing his weekly cleaning while entertaining anyone who stops by. We stop in the living room where I can sit next to her as we look out the window at the construction of a new wing on the building. The increased demand for nursing care and assisted living, now fifteen years after the retirement community opened, is evident.

Although I can't bring my dog in to lunch with us, I retrieve her after lunch for a visit with Mom, who welcomes her and reaches down to pat her soft white fur. She is the same breed as my parents' last dog and fills, for me and Mom, that human need for unconditional love. She also brings out Mom's obsession with the safety and welfare of these four-legged friends. "Where's the dog? Is she OK? She's not eating anything, is she?" I assure her that all is well—the dog is lying under the table. Mom starts to wheel herself toward the door (her arm strength and coordination have stuck with her a bit) and signals it's time to move on.

Once settled back in her bed—an ordeal that requires two nurses and a Hoyer lift—I cover her with her fleece blanket and sit hoping I can keep her attention just a little longer.

"So, Mom. Back when you were seven and on that vacation at the beach, the girl you met had a dog, right?"

Amazing! She's listening! "Yes. His name was Hobbs. He was a Swiss Mountain dog, a big dog, and he went everywhere with Peanut."

"Peanut?"

"No, Hobbs."

Mom seems to remember more about the dog than anything—not that I'm surprised.

"Was Peanut the girl who collected seaweed on the beach? Did you keep in touch with her after your vacation was over?"

"Janey was jealous. My sister. She's here, isn't she? I want to see my sister."

What do I say now? The truth. If I can give nothing else to her, I can give her the truth.

"No, Mom. Janey is not here. She died thirteen years ago, but I'm sure she's close to you in your heart."

"Where's the dog?"

"Mine? Oh, she's right here. She's fine."

Silence. She is asleep. Time for me to leave.

JIM

*B*orn in 1910 in Portland on Maine's southern coast, Jim was what most would describe as a "regular kind of guy."

He was the oldest of three children who enjoyed an upper-middle-class upbringing in the state's largest city—a small city by national standards, but large enough to afford a young family with stable employment, a comfortable home in a safe, friendly neighborhood, good schools, and all of the daily conveniences. He was fortunate that his father's job was steady and allowed his mother to be a full-time mom. She adored her children, Jim and his two sisters, two and four years younger than he.

Jim's father was an only child and also grew up in the Portland area. His father, Jim's grandfather (and yes, they were all named James in the fashion of the day), had done well during the second industrial revolution of the 1880s and the westward expansion of the railroad. During that time, over 7,000 miles of new track were laid each year, and together with the invention of electricity and the adoption of standard time zones, the industry was among the fastest growing and strongest in the nation. Jim's grandfather's work required extensive travel and time away from home, but his in-laws lived nearby and ensured that his son, born in 1890, and his wife were never alone.

James Sr. had always envisioned a large family, but his wife's ill health resulted in only one successful birth. His son, his only child, was his pride and joy. He raised him with the highest standards, teaching him the values of compassion, commitment, hard work, and purpose. Later in life, long after his working days were over, James Sr. relished watching his son marry, secure a good job of his own, and become a father himself. In many ways, his own dreams were fulfilled through the life of his son. He was truly blessed.

One of those dreams was to provide his family with access to the sea. James Sr.'s world was largely landlocked, yet from a young age, he developed a powerful attraction to the expansive ocean beyond the eastern edge of the city. The sea was always nearby but at the same time, so far away. He and his wife, and later his son's family, had modest homes in the northwest section of Portland, near the Windham town line. It was a rural environment, largely farmland, yet an easy trolley or carriage ride into the city for work. Views to the west were dominated by the peak of Mt. Washington in neighboring New Hampshire. To the east lay the city and beyond its busy streets, the shores of Casco Bay and the Atlantic.

The only time either James Sr. or his son and their families ever experienced the life of the nearby seacoast was on their occasional trips to the fish market on Portland harbor's Commercial Street. From there one could admire (and smell!) the working piers that were home to hundreds of cargo and fishing boats and enjoy expansive views of Casco Bay and its many islands. To the south, the coastline opened up to long sandy beaches. To the north, a more rugged landscape was dominated by wooded peninsulas and rocky shores. Smaller towns and villages spread out in all directions around Portland, a well-established East Coast metropolis of the time, only 120 miles north of Boston and connected by a well-developed and growing system of transportation both by land and sea.

In 1897, James Sr. was 32 years old and well into his lucrative career with the railroad. He had been married for nine years, and his son, James Jr., was seven. That was also the year that the Higgins Beach Realty Company was formed. The company took ownership of a large saltwater farm abutting the ocean in the town of Scarborough, five miles south of Portland. The property had been owned for generations by the Higgins family, most recently by Hiram Higgins, who had inherited the 150 acres from his father in the 1870s. Hiram died in 1891, and his children, who recognized the recent boom of tourism along Maine's extensive coastline and lacked interest in carrying on the family's commitment to farming, subdivided the land into an arrangement of streets and house lots. From 1900 to 1910, the Higgins Beach community came to be, a picturesque seaside grouping of summer cottages, inns, and a general store.

Somewhat on a whim, James Sr. decided that an investment in a small beachfront lot would be a good way to put away some of his earnings. He purchased one on what was to become Cliff Street, the most elevated section of Higgins Beach on its southern end. The year was 1901, and already a number of small cottages had popped up along the shoreline, typically two-story, wood-shingled bungalows, with footprints allowing for modest accommodations. Young families began to emerge for summer picnics and bonfires on the beach. By 1903, a general store called The Pavilion had opened, and soon thereafter, vacationing tourists from all over New England began to discover this little gem on the coast of Maine. James Sr. seemed to have made a good decision, and although he had yet to build on his lot, his family had unlimited access to a new "playground" just a few miles from home.

James Sr. never did build on the property, but for years it was well used for day trips out of the city. James Jr.'s childhood became defined by these excursions. When he married in 1909 at the age of 19, his father gave him and his bride the property as their wedding gift, and James immediately began drawing up plans for a house—the house that his son, Jim, and two daughters would grow up in.

EARLY APRIL 2017

Each of my visits with Mom over the past ten months has also included time with Dad. He still lives in their beautiful independent living apartment on the first floor of the three-story building with huge windows looking out to the ocean. He is just across the driveway and an easy walk from Mom's room in the adjoining health center. He never misses his 4 p.m. visit with her, although, by all reports, he regularly joins in her nap before she is awakened and taken off to dinner.

Today, I follow my normal routine—find a place to park, which is usually a challenge, gather any groceries I may have picked up for Dad in one hand (or use the cart at the door if I have more than one bag and especially if I have a twelve-pack of Samuel Adams Boston Lager), let my dog out of the car, and make my way to Dad's apartment. As expected, he's in his chair, eyes closed, comfies on, coffee cup on the table at his side. When he realizes I'm there, I receive a warm greeting as he gets kisses from my dog. She stays with him as I venture off, Dad's trash and recycling in hand, to see Mom.

For her entire life, Mom has been an avid photographer. What distinguishes her, however, is her impeccable attention to organizing and preserving her photographs. At last count, she had sixty-two albums dating from the 1940s to 2012. Five years ago, many things began to change, and along with jigsaw puzzles and driving, organizing photographs went by the wayside.

Just a week ago, we had brought one of the bookshelves full of Mom's photographs from the apartment to her room to have them handy to look at with her. Her albums are big, heavy, and quite difficult to hold, so I had purchased a music stand for that purpose. (It works beautifully!)

Mom is asleep when I arrive—it's about 11 a.m.—but, as usual, all it takes is a soft "hello, Mom" and her eyes open, a smile graces her face, and, to my incredible joy I hear, "Hello, Kathy dear." (Sometimes her sleep wins out but not often.)

"I've come to have lunch with you."

"Oh, I must get up."

"Are you hungry?"

"I'm *always* hungry!"

And so we begin our visit with a laugh. What more could I ask for?

Today, as we leave the dining room after lunch, Mom makes it clear that she wants to go back to her *zimmer*. *Zimmer*, you ask? Why, her room, of course: *zimmer* is German for *room*—one of Mom's favorite German words, along with *waschlappen* (*washcloth*)—a language she learned from her mother and during the year she spent as a child in Switzerland.

Back in her *zimmer*, there are few options. It seems a shame to have her go right back to bed, so I position the music stand next to her wheelchair and pull out a photo album. It happens to be my favorite. When my parents moved here after fifty-five years in Connecticut, downsizing quite a bit (to say the least!), Mom literally unframed dozens of framed photographs (she had a collage frame for every year of our lives) and put them all in one album.

She recognizes most of what is before her—a section of beautiful, obviously professional baby pictures for each of the three children, annual memories of summers in Quogue (the most wonderful little village on the beach on Long Island where we enjoyed the best summers anyone could ever ask for), images (many!) of her various dogs over the years, records of ski vacations, our trip to a dude ranch in Wyoming in 1966, hanging our stockings with care *every* Christmas, and so much more. Many of the photos had been enlarged for framing, so as we revisit them today, she can actually see them.

Turning the pages slowly for her, I cherish the moment and am calmed by the fact that so many memories are there. You just have to know how to find them (particularly the nude portrait I took of her in the 1970s as a birthday gift for my dad!).

"Oh, my gosh! Mom! Look at this," I react with excitement as I turn a page and there, right before us, is a beautiful photograph of Mom and her sister with a caption, in her distinctive

30

handwriting: *Janey and Annie, March 1932* (just months before their beach vacation in Maine).

The sepia photo is classic: two young girls with shoulder-length hair beautifully combed and pinned on one side with a large ribbon bow. Their matching short-sleeved frocks remind me of the children dressed alike in *The Sound of Music*. Annie is gently resting her head on Janey's shoulder, both girls looking directly at the camera; most definitely a formal photo shoot but characterized by its simplicity. Although I sense a sternness in Janey's eyes, Annie's are warm, almost sleepy, so peaceful.

In my moments of awe and close inspection of this wonderful image, Mom has drifted. I reach for the call bell, and Sarah arrives with Mike and they carefully move Mom to her bed. "Thank you," I smile as I leave, feeling so very grateful for the wonderful care Mom receives and the knowledge that I can go home and not worry about her.

SUNDAY, JULY 17, 1932

*O*n a normal Sunday morning in the city, Annie and Janey would be awakened early, fed a light breakfast, and dressed in their Sunday best for church. The routine was so ingrained in them that both girls woke up early this Sunday morning to the rising sun, only to fall back on their pillows in laughter. This Sunday they did not have to go to church. In fact, they didn't have to do anything but savor the simplicity and freedom of this wonderful escape.

The inn served a full brunch on Sundays, later than the regular breakfast, so there was no rush to get up. Annie was tired.

When she'd gone to the bathroom just before bed, something very strange had caught her eye and kept her awake for a long time. At first, it had been just a quick flicker of light in the far distance, visible through the bedroom window that faced east. Thinking nothing of it, Annie had gone back to bed but had then soon seen more light coming from offshore in periodic flashes. Unable to get her bearings, she had not been able to tell exactly where the flashes were coming from, but they had seemed to be in some odd sense of order. One long beam, three quick flashes, pause, one long flash, pause, five quick flashes, stop. A boat in distress? Lost in the fog? Something on land? Her imagination ran wild.

Descending the stairs for brunch, Bill, Annie, and Janey beamed as they saw rows of waves glistening under a totally blue sky and gently rolling onto the white sand of the beach, a welcome change from the day before. It promised to be an ideal summer day, their third full day of vacation, a day to stay put and enjoy nature's playground right outside their door. The inn provided an umbrella, and Bill ordered a basket of fruit, cheese, and bread so they could head down to the beach for the entire day.

Although Bill remained in his casual street clothes, the girls donned their swimsuits and hoped for the courage to test the cool Maine ocean water. Picking their spot on the beach, they quickly set up camp amidst constant excited chatter and giggles.

"Pa! Look at all the people here today! Is it OK if I go explore? Can I talk to the other people? Anyone I want?" Typical Annie!

With a smile and a nod, Bill released her into a day so perfect that all thoughts of the day before—Jim, Peanut, the city, the mysterious nighttime lights—fell away. This was a day of sand castles, splashing in the waves, chasing seagulls with the other children, collecting seashells, and even a bit of sunbathing with the soft afternoon sea breeze gently caressing her skin. Annie was in virtual heaven!

Janey preferred to stay in the shade of the umbrella, and Bill left the beach for a bit, feeling confident that the girls were safe and quite content. This was all he'd ever hoped for—time to witness the differing personalities emerging from his precious children as they enjoyed the freedom of this day—and he relished what he saw.

BILL

*B*ill Walling was a proud man, not only of his two daughters but of his service to his country. After his college years at Hamilton (class of 1917, non-graduate) and subsequent studies at the School of Military Aeronautics in Illinois, Bill served as an Army Signal Corps officer during World War I. His command was as pilot in the Lafayette Escadrille, a group of American aviators who enlisted in the French Army before the U.S. entered the war. (Years later he would go on to achieve medals of distinction in World War II.)

One of four children, Bill was born and raised in Upstate New York and laid claim, on his mother's side, to Mayflower heritage. He was also very proud of the Medal of Honor that had been passed down to him by his paternal grandfather, Capt. William Henry Walling, whose gallantry earned him the award from the Union Army at Fort Fisher, North Carolina, during the Civil War. A lot for Bill to live up to.

Bill loved to tell stories to his girls and often dug into his family history to do so.

"Annie Pannie, would you ever like to visit France?"

"Why France? You know I would go anywhere with you, but *France*? It's so far away."

"Well, a few years ago, I was there. In fact, when World War I ended, I was in Paris and there was a spectacular celebration. It really is a wonderful place."

"What were you doing in France? During a war? Weren't you scared?"

"I flew airplanes and helped France win the war. You see, our country and France are good friends. I was there to do what I could to help—and I love to fly, so it wasn't all that bad. The only hard part was missing my family and not being able to come home for holidays."

"How old were you when you were in France?"

"In my early twenties. About the same age as our new friend, Jim. I was in college but wanted to serve my country. So I did."

"Didn't your parents try to stop you? They must have been scared to lose you."

"Well, I grew up with what we call 'Walling blood.' My parents always told me, 'As long as you don't hurt anyone, you should pursue what you want to do, not what others think you are supposed to do. Live a life of honesty, gaiety, and courage!' I hold my parents' lessons close to my heart and now get to share them with you."

"Sounds good to me! You want to know what I want to do when I grow up?"

"Sure, as long as it's something honorable."

"Well, actually, I have no idea!"

While in France, Bill kept in touch with his family, who had, by then, moved to Great Neck, Long Island. He was an avid letter writer, sending reports of his daily activities in the war—flying being his true passion—home to his parents and siblings.

He missed Thanksgiving and Christmas in 1918, but with few regrets. He was doing exactly what he wanted to do.

Now, over a decade later, he was again doing exactly what he wanted to do: being a father to two budding young ladies whose lives lay ahead of them, lives he hoped to help shape through his unconditional love, guidance, and support.

MID-APRIL 2017

*M*om's condition seems quite stable, not improving but also not progressing. I spend more time with Dad now—he is being challenged by a recurrent urinary problem— and I worry a lot about his being alone, increasingly losing his eyesight and ability to walk, sleeping much more, and struggling with many of his daily routines. I make his bed now. I often get him breakfast. I make sure I am there when he showers. I can tell in my inspection of the apartment that he has stumbled or fallen. Staff and residents continually ask me about him and gently express their concern about his safety. He really should not be alone.

There is a shortage of available apartments in assisted living, and since January, I have had to appeal for consideration of Dad's situation and needs. It has been a challenge, but finally he has been selected to move to assisted living; an apartment will be available for him in mid-May. With his move, however, will come the task of emptying the apartment my parents have lived in for twelve years and all that comes with that (a story for another book!).

This "distraction" takes away from my time with Mom and will continue to do so for the next month. I manage to see her, but feel torn between my time with her and my Dad. She loves my visits, but I know that she is in good care, and she doesn't seem to be aware of my increasing absences.

A new pattern in our visits is emerging. Her willingness to be transferred from her bed to the wheelchair creates increasing anxiety, and I often encounter her tears after the nurses have completed their task.

Deep breath. "What's the matter, Mom?" I sit on her bed facing her, forcing myself into a calmness that I hope she can feel and join me in. Quiet. Another deep breath. "It's OK, Mom. Let's go get some lunch."

She doesn't look happy, but I move on until I hear her soft voice.

"I have a secret to tell you. You promise you won't tell anyone?"

"Of course. What is it?"

"Well, I have a plan. I am going to get out of here, and no one is going to know."

"Really?" I lean over to listen, hiding my smile, relishing her characteristic determination. "And where will you go?"

"Away from here—where I belong."

"Well, I think that's great."

"Promise you won't tell anyone! Promise!"

"Of course not—you know you can trust me."

Laughing gently inside, I continue to push her to the dining room. Having told me her secret, she is calm; the anxiety has passed as if nothing had ever bothered her. We have lunch. We walk the hallways a bit and check out progress on the construction through the activity room window. As usual, we are greeted by other residents, staff, visitors, and caregivers passing by— Sandy, Ralph, Ruth, Jessica, Linda, Brian, Bob, Irene, Charlotte, Dick, Deborah, Chris...—but Mom, who used to embrace everyone and every conversation, seems to want to move on, back to her room, back to the safety of her bed, her sleep, alone.

SUNDAY, JULY 17, 1932, 5 P.M.

After serving a large brunch on Sundays, dinner at the inn was a small buffet of cold cuts, soup, sliced vegetables, and an assortment of fruit and sweets. Enjoying the dramatic colors of the slowly setting sun, Bill, Janey, and Annie helped themselves and settled in on the porch for a quiet evening.

"Boy, I did nothing today and I am exhausted!" Annie declared.

"That's what fresh air and sunshine will do to you," Bill responded, all smiles. "It's the best medicine anyone could ever ask for."

Janey quietly sipped her lemonade and turned a page of her book. She wished she had the same energy as her little sister. She had enjoyed her day on the beach, but she never felt comfortable joining in with the other children as she had watched Annie do so effortlessly.

"Did you see Jim or Peanut today, Annie dear?"

"No, I didn't. I was so busy having fun, I didn't even look for them. It's Sunday, so maybe they went to church or had other things to do. Jim did say he was going to see some friends while he was here. I have no idea what Peanut and her father do on Sundays—probably rest!"

"Hey, Pa, did you bring that special game you're so good at—the one that Mother told us you're so famous for? She said you're the New York City champ, and you wrote a book about it, right?"

True admiration shone in Bill's glance when he looked at Janey. She had remembered his recent accomplishment.

"Backgammon? Yes, I did bring a board hoping I might teach you both how to play. Would you like to give it a try? It can actually be very challenging, but the basics are easy to learn."

Absorbed in sorting her day's collection of shells, Annie ignored this exchange and enjoyed her solitude while Bill taught Janey the game that had made him quite notable in New York circles. He proudly used illustrations from his book, *Backgammon Standards*, published just the year before, to help her set up the board.

Janey placed the black and white men on the board, fifteen each, as shown in Bill's diagram. Each player had their own set of dice and threw one apiece to see who would go first. As they began, Janey thought it did seem rather simple. "So, I just need to move all my men to this corner of the board and then take them off? And, you do the same thing going the other direction?"

Chuckling, Bill acknowledged that yes, that was the point, and the game ensued. With her father and sister fully absorbed, Annie wandered into the inn, where guests were scattered about reading, napping, and quietly engaged in conversation. Nothing too exciting going on in there, and there was still enough daylight for a short walk on the beach.

"Pa, can I go on the beach for a little bit? It's still light and I won't go far—I'll stay where you can see me."

"I'd rather you stay close, dearie. How about you just walk to the top of the road and back? Here—you can take the field glasses with you. You can get a good look at the beach with these, maybe even see the houses out there on the point."

Annie suddenly felt very special as Bill handed her the black metal and morocco leather field glasses—and quite grown up being given permission to go off on her own. Wandering the beach was one thing, but being given freedom to explore the street alone was another. She took it quite seriously.

"I promise to stay on this road only, and I will be back before the sun sets," she promised.

The road was very short, and she passed only three small cottages before reaching the woods. A slight rise in the terrain offered an entirely different perspective of the beach. In awe, she found a large boulder at the edge of the woods where she settled herself and began to take in the nearly 360-degree view around her.

Tall pine trees lined the woods next to her on rocky ledges that reached down to the sea. The tide lapped against the black stone, and seagulls dove on the clam shells left on shore as the tide receded. The beach extended almost as far as she could see, empty now as the warm summer day drew to a close. Along the shoreline, the dirt road separated the beach from a line of shingled cottages. *Which one did Jim grow up in?* Annie wondered as she recalled their bike ride and conversation of the day before.

Reminded of Peanut's story, her eyes were drawn to the point of land extending into the sea in the distance. There were two houses—one tucked in the woods, the other more exposed on the end of the point. The tree—yes, it looked like an umbrella—stood next to the second house, which, Annie realized, must be Peanut's. Focusing the field glasses, she could make out the lines of a small farmhouse, two stories, with a nice porch and detached shed. What surprised her, however, was the three-story tower at one end of the house with windows along the top floor—quite similar to the tower at the inn, but a strange addition to this otherwise simple home. If *she* lived there, that's where she would want her bedroom to be!

More carefully scanning the coastline, now that she had figured out how to focus the field glasses, Annie spotted some activity where the river separated the beach from the peninsula. A small boat was coming across, and she could see two small figures on the beach walking toward it. And, with a closer look, a dog. Inching herself along the rock as if to get closer to what she was seeing, Annie watched carefully: a boat landing on the shore, a person getting off, three figures getting into the boat, a dog jumping in behind them, the boat moving away toward the peninsula on the other side of the river.

The sun was quickly setting (how fast it happens in those last minutes before it fully disappears!) and Annie got up to return to the inn. Curiosity filled her thoughts. Maybe that was Jim, Peanut, and Hobbs catching a ride from the beach to Peanut's house? Sure would be quicker than traveling by land to get there.

Back at the inn, with just a touch of daylight left, Annie took one last look through the field glasses. There—the boat was back on the beach. But no one was around. Panning a bit closer, two figures appeared, walking her way on the beach. The third person—and the dog—were not there.

"Annie dear!" Bill's voice rang clearly from a window above.

"I'm back, Pa. I'll be right in."

Climbing quickly up the stairs, Annie relished her possible discovery: Jim and someone with a boat giving Peanut and Hobbs a ride home from the beach on this quiet Sunday evening?

PEANUT

Her father never missed her that afternoon. Typically, on Sundays he retreated to his room and buried himself in paperwork that Peanut surmised had something to do with money. Sundays were the one day that she was free to come and go as she pleased as long as she stayed on the property. What

Peanut had discovered, however, was that whether she went off into their neighboring fields or woods, or escaped to the beach beyond her permitted boundaries, it didn't really matter as long as she was back in the house by dark. Her father never really paid that much attention.

Announcing her return, Peanut was greeted by a low mumble, her father now solidly placed in his armchair, a half-full bottle at his side, the radio on with tunes of Jack Benny adding a touch of life to the room. She lit the lantern in the kitchen to see what her father had left behind for her to clean up. Dirty dishes, some food scraps, a couple of empty beer bottles—nothing out of the ordinary. After feeding Hobbs the scraps, she busied herself cleaning up the rest and preparing a meal of chowder and biscuits for dinner. She would eat hers alone in the kitchen and bring her father's to him in the front room before heading up to bed. Little was said between them. Their routine was quite set and required little conversation. It would be hard for most fifteen-year-old girls living alone with their father, tending to all the household chores, having no one to talk to or play with, adhering to the strictest of rules. But Peanut had no choice. What she did have was Jim.

Peanut couldn't quite remember when and how she had met Jim, but for as long as she could remember, he had been her one and only true friend. Yes, there were boys and girls at school, and she did have a few cousins who lived nearby. But she had always been an outsider, different, rejected. It had all become very obvious and hurtful four years earlier when she lost her mother. She had never been told how her mother died and had felt like an outcast ever since. Whispers. Whispers. It seemed as if there was something everyone knew except her. It made her feel ashamed, afraid, vulnerable. The only person who seemed to accept her, to befriend her, was Jim, a boy she had met at her uncle's horse farm years before. A boy who didn't judge her. A boy who loved to talk, to listen, to explore. A boy who wasn't afraid to bend the rules—as long as it didn't cause any harm.

The adventures that Peanut had shared with Jim over the years were many. At first, when she was but a little girl and he was not yet a teenager, they had found pleasure climbing trees, running in the fields, mucking through the riverbed at low tide, and joining in with summer visitors at the beach. Jim's younger sister often trailed along, and Peanut saw them as the brother and sister she had never had. They embraced her; she relished their friendship. Not unlike others who were fortunate to grow up on the beach, summertime defined Peanut's childhood, and summertime meant Jim.

LATE APRIL 2017

With all that's going on with Dad recently, my visits with Mom continue to lessen. UTIs are the nemesis of old age, I have discovered! Drink your water! Delusions, pain, confusion, trips to the emergency room (which never go quickly). It happened with Mom; now it's happening with Dad. Only a couple more weeks and he will move to assisted living, which should make things much easier for everyone.

Mom carries on. The routine remains the same. Phyllis is back from Florida but unfortunately wearing a neck brace due to a fall she took down there. Mary's husband has passed on, but she remains the life of the party at lunch. Anna remains quiet and seemingly bothered by something. Mom's leaning, always to the right, has her nearly falling over and I compensate, unconsciously, by leaning to the left.

I have been busy emptying Mom and Dad's apartment, sorting through clothing, books, paperwork, dishes, linens, and the endless assortment of collectibles that one accumulates over the years. My parents downsized considerably when they moved here twelve years ago, but the apartment with its two bedrooms, living/dining room, kitchen, two bathrooms, and three large closets is a project not to be minimized. The real challenge, however, is that every single thing I touch brings back a memory and causes me to run through the same series of questions: Move it to assisted living for Dad? Pack it away carefully to store and deal with later? Leave it for my sister or brother to decide? Figure out how to get it to one of the grandchildren, or keep it for myself? Pack it up for the thrift shop? Throw it away? It is a very slow, deliberate process, and I try to work through it discreetly so that Dad is largely unaware of what I am up to. I don't want this rather disruptive and confusing stage of his life to upset him any more than it has to. I feel very responsible—this is my parents' *life*! At least there is one thing I don't have to think about—selling anything. Dad responded quickly when I asked him what I should do with the things that no one could use. Without hesitation he declared, "Give it to charity"—a clear message that actually made my job a bit easier.

As I take my time tackling this seemingly endless task, my dog is staring at me. I do wish she could help, but at least she's patient. One or two hours at a time is all I can handle. And oh, the dust!

Fortunately, this process does have its lighter moments. Pulling a beach towel out from Mom's closet shelf, I jump back in amazement as twenty-dollar bills start drifting to the floor. "Oh my God, Dad!" I run to his bathroom, where he is shaving. "You won't believe what I just found! Mom's hidden stash—two hundred dollars!"

"We should give it to her," Dad says without hesitation.

"But you know, Dad, she doesn't need any money now. Shouldn't I just put it with your cash?"

"No, dear. It's your mother's money, not mine to take."

"Well, I could put it in her bank account, if that's what you want. She still has one." And that is exactly what I did.

Mom was never one for makeup, jewelry, or dressing up, but she and Dad did have a social life over the years, and there were times when she would pull out a string of pearls or her scarab pin and bracelet. Growing up, I always gazed with wonder at the small arrangement of jewelry carefully laid out on top of her bureau. She did that when they moved here, too, but eventually I told her that, with the cleaning lady and others in and out of the apartment, it was probably best to put things away. So, in packing, I find multiple little boxes with assorted pins, rings, necklaces, and watches—nothing of great value but clearly many memories. Nothing is thrown away; it all goes into the "Mom—Do Not Throw Away" box.

There is one piece of jewelry that I've never seen before, and it makes me pause. It's a very small, simple shell—a clam shell, I think—carefully strung on a piece of worn ribbon. It's wrapped in old, weathered paper tissue, obviously a treasure from long ago. Mom is known to date and organize almost everything, but I see no clue here. I could take it over to her room and ask her about it, but, as with many other tidbits I have run into along the way, it will have to remain a mystery and join the rest in the Do Not Throw Away box for another day.

MONDAY, JULY 18, 1932

Another beautiful day greeted Annie as she awoke to a warm breeze filling the room. Feeling rather settled in this now familiar environment, she lay quietly absorbing the tranquility surrounding her. In the city, she would typically wake up to the crashing noises of the early-morning garbage trucks and the increasing hum of cars traveling up and down Fifth Avenue. Now, the only noise she could hear was the squawking of gulls and the low rumblings of people moving about in the dining room below.

In two days, she would turn seven! Did Pa even remember? It really didn't matter that much because this trip alone was the best birthday present anyone could ever have given her.

Her thoughts drifted, and startled, she jumped from her bed to the window. It had happened again, she remembered. Last night. A clear, moonless night had beckoned her to the window. The stars were amazing! She did recognize a couple of constellations—the easiest to find was always Orion, his belt and sword clearly on display in the southeastern sky. In the city, the lights of the buildings and streets prevented her from seeing the stars, but she had spent a couple of summers with her mother's family in Cooperstown, New York, where stargazing was a regular nighttime activity with her cousins. The most fun had been lying in the grass patiently waiting for a shooting star to pass overhead. Cooperstown held a special place in her heart, and she would be going there again next month. For now, though, she focused back on the beach and remembered what else she had seen late last night.

Flashing lights in the distance—again, now two nights in a row. She struggled to remember. It had been a pattern, just like the night before but different this time. Four quick flashes. Pause. One quick flash. One more and then a long one. Two more quick ones. Pause. What next? Yes, one more quick one, two long, one quick. So strange. They had come from the same direction as before but were much clearer, and Annie was surprised by how easily she remembered the order. No paper. No pencil in the room. Annie scrambled to get dressed and ran down to the sitting room so she could write down what she had seen. Tucking the small piece of paper in her pocket, she returned to her room to wake her sister.

"Janey!" She shook her sister urgently. "Wake up! I have to tell you something! Janey!"

With a grumble, Janey rolled over and squinted at the morning sun beaming through the window.

"What on earth do you want, Annie? Can't you wait? You're always so dramatic! What is it?" Irritated, Janey rose to sit on the side of her bed.

Just then, Bill knocked gently on the door and called out, "Everything OK in there?"

Annie opened the door for her father, who glanced curiously around the room. Everything seemed in order—no intruders, no injuries, no apparent reason for Annie's excitement.

"So what's going on at this early hour?"

"Pa, I saw the strangest thing out the window last night. I didn't tell you, but I saw it the night before, too."

"What did you see? And what were you doing up in the middle of the night?"

Motioning Annie to join him on the bed, Bill sat, gently rubbing Janey's back as they made an effort to listen seriously to whatever Annie had to reveal.

"Well, I couldn't sleep, and I could see stars through the window so I got up. I found Orion—remember that one, Janey?"

"Yeah, it's the easiest to find. Did you find the Milky Way?"

"No. But I did see flashing lights coming from somewhere over the ocean."

"What kind of lights were they, dearie?" Bill asked attempting to be as serious as possible.

"They were bigger than the stars. A lot bigger! And they all came from the same place—in order."

"In order? What do you mean by that?" Bill sat up a bit straighter, showing more serious interest in Annie's revelation while Janey lay back down and pulled the covers over her head.

"I wrote it down. See?" Annie pulled the paper from her pocket and handed it to Bill.

"Some of the flashes were very quick and others lasted a few seconds. It was strange. It was almost as if it was a secret message in the sky."

Rising and walking to the window, Bill looked down at Annie's scribbles, up out the window, and back to Annie. "Where exactly did these lights come from?"

"Over there somewhere." Annie pointed to the open sea. "Maybe that island out there. Or maybe a little bit that way." Her arm turned a bit to the left, more toward the land than the ocean.

Being only six, yet quickly approaching seven, Annie's written words were limited. All that Bill saw on her paper was a series of S's and L's.

"Annie, dear. What do these letters stand for?"

"Short and long. Some of the flashes lasted longer. It was weird, almost as if they were trying to tell me something. Well, probably not me but someone."

A slow, thoughtful *hmm* emerged from Bill. Could it be? He had seen it used during the war as a form of communication: Morse code. He didn't know the code, but he was pretty sure it was based on dots and dashes—short and long. Maybe someone here was using it for some reason, and this piqued his curiosity.

"Well, Annie dear. I really don't know what this could be, but I'll check with the innkeepers today and find out if they have seen this. My guess is that it's coming from a boat offshore. Nothing to be concerned about. Janey, why don't you get up, and we can go down for breakfast. Looks like we have another fine day ahead."

It took no time at all for the girls to resume their beach routine from the day before. Bill excused himself, for he had a mis-

sion at hand. Walking back to the inn's kitchen after the breakfast shift had ended, he wandered about hoping to find the
innkeepers. Unsuccessful, he decided to see if Jim was about
and climbed the three flights of stairs to the tower room. No
one answered his knock, the hallway was empty, and everyone
appeared to have headed out for the day. His curiosity would
have to be put aside for now.

Grabbing the field glasses from his room, Bill headed to
the shaded porch for the remainder of the morning. The 10
a.m. low tide, a couple of hours later than on their first morning, opened up the wide stretch of sand now populated by the
summer beachgoers. He had the porch to himself and sat con-
templating the possibilities of what Annie had witnessed. She
did have an exceptional imagination, but this seemed to have
some real truth to it. He looked at the paper again. Four S's—
space—one S—space—one S, one L, two S's—space—one S,
two L's, one S. It had to be Morse code, or something similar,
but what did it say? Who sent it? From where? For whom?

Looking through the glasses, Bill panned the horizon. To
the left, cottages lined the beach up to the river. Across the river
was largely farmland edged by the woods. Two houses stood
out on the peninsula. A small island edged the shore where the
sea opened to the vast horizon. No boats. Bill did remember
hearing that the waters here were very shallow, and other than
small skiffs and dories, water traffic was limited within two to
three miles out. It was a peaceful scene. It must have been a
cargo ship approaching Portland Harbor, sending a message of
arrival. But with Portland to the north and around the point,
why would the lights have been so visible from here?

Bill's contemplation was interrupted by the sound of cry-
ing. He was alone on the porch, and the inn had emptied out
after breakfast. Turning slowly, he peered through the door and
caught a glimpse of two people, arm in arm, ascending the
stairs. One appeared to be wrapped in a blanket. They disap-

peared around the landing leading to the second floor. Hopefully no one is hurt, Bill thought, returning his attention to the beach where his daughters were playing.

Moments later, the porch door opened and Jim appeared with a look that reminded Bill of his war days. He saw and sensed fear and pain as Jim stood silently in the doorway.

"Jim. Everything all right?"

No response. Jim looked cautiously at Bill and turned back into the inn.

It was an awkward moment. Something must be terribly wrong, Bill thought. He barely knew Jim. Yes, they had spent part of a day together, and Jim had entertained Annie on a bike ride. He was a nice young man and seemed quite capable. Bill wondered if he should persist and see what was going on. Whatever was happening was certainly none of his business. And Jim had walked away.

Sitting back, Bill waited a few minutes before entering the inn himself. This he could not ignore. He found Jim alone, sitting in the corner with his head buried in his hands. Approaching slowly, Bill stopped short when Jim lifted his head, tears running down his face.

"Whatever happened, Jim? What's wrong?" Bill walked across the room and took a seat next to Jim. "Was that you helping someone upstairs? Is someone hurt? Can I help?"

"You remember my friend Peanut?"

"Sure. I met her at the market. Is she OK?"

"Well, she had a rough night last night, and I brought her here so she could get some rest. We're very close friends. We grew up together."

"Yes, Annie told me a bit about both of you after her bike ride the other day. Is there anything I can do to help? You look like you could use something to cheer you up. I'm not doing anything at the moment if you want to talk. The girls are content on the beach. I can leave you be if you'd rather."

Jim stared out the window trying to collect himself. Bill could feel his pain and it was deep. It was difficult to witness.

"Let's go on the porch," Jim suggested. "I could use some fresh air."

They sat down, and after a moment, Jim said, "That's Peanut's house over there." He pointed to the peninsula in the distance. "She lives there with her father. Her mother died four years ago. I grew up with Peanut. She's like a little sister to me."

Bill sat and listened quietly as Jim continued. His story was painful and raw.

Jim described the two things that had defined his life so far—his blessed childhood upbringing here on the shores of the Atlantic and the untimely death of his oldest sister fourteen years before.

JIM

The oldest of three children, he being the only boy, Jim had been a fun-loving, responsible, healthy, and happy child—a picture of perfection, some might say. His two sisters were two and four years younger and he took his older-brother responsibilities very seriously. They were siblings but also the best of friends.

Jim's parents had provided their children with a secure, nurturing upbringing. Their winters were spent in a cozy home in Portland and their summers at the cottage at Higgins Beach.

"My dad has always been the most proud of the cottage he built here. It was so hard for him to sell and leave, but with the economy as it has been recently, I guess he had no choice. My parents sold the place two years ago and moved to Michigan where my dad got a great job," Jim began. "He ordered a Sears kit house. Have you heard of them?" Bill nodded as Jim continued. "A two-story foursquare. One of the most popular styles. He loves to describe the day it arrived, as he liked to make us believe, in a box! My dad is quite the storyteller—always has been, especially after his evening cocktail." Jim finally produced a hint of a smile as Bill listened attentively.

Jim re-told his father's story of building their Higgins Beach cottage, the kit house, and how it had been finished just in time for the birth of his first child, Jim. He went on to describe his childhood. Although he spoke of his school days and Portland neighborhood friends, Jim's most enduring memories were of his summers at the beach. They were idyllic. Jim and his sisters experienced a childhood of freedom and fresh air. The community was about as safe as any to be found, and once you learned to ride a bike, you gained unmatched independence. Jim's mother took the kids to the cottage as soon as school let out, and they stayed the entire summer. Jim's father joined them on weekends and during his three-week summer vacation. The children's days followed a simple pattern: up with the sun, breakfast, morning chores, off to the beach or on the bikes for the day, only stopping in at some point for lunch and making sure they were home for dinner promptly at 6.

As one who leaned toward spoiling his daughters, Bill inquired, "Chores? What did you have to do?"

"Oh, it wasn't much. I swept the stairs and outside porch; Lucy, my oldest sister, made sandwiches for lunch so they were easy to grab whenever we wanted; and Mandy took out the trash. And yes, we always had to make our beds. Mom never let us get away without making sure we had done our daily duties."

Not much, Bill thought, but a good way to instill a sense of responsibility at a young age.

"Did you have a lot of friends?"

"Why yes!" Jim exclaimed. "The best of friends—most are still around. We're like one big family around here. It's very special. I expect we'll all be friends for life. Hopefully we will."

Jim's memory of the better times in his life seemed to have exploded, and Bill enjoyed his enthusiasm. Descriptions of what he called Junior Sports and the annual Field Day took Bill back to his own childhood and summer games with his friends—relay races, high-jumping competitions, softball toss, three-legged races—with Jim just adding a few games unique to Higgins Beach, like lobster trap pulling and seaweed tossing.

Then there was the general store, The Pavilion. Bill had been there that one time on their first day and sensed that it was the center of town, but Jim's recollections confirmed so much more. Candy and ice cream you could *charge*! A really big deal if your parents allowed it. For Jim and his sisters, it was limited to one treat a week, more restrictive than for most of their friends, but they never complained. Nighttime occasionally led to a raid on the candy counter. The back window of the store was rarely locked, but it only took being caught once for that activity to stop! And the Saturday night dances! Although for the adults only (you had to be over 18 to attend), the music could be heard blocks away, and Jim often snuck around with his buddies after dark to spy on the activity. The last thing Jim mentioned before turning sullen again were the family bonfires on the beach at night, a real weekend treat when all the dads, full of song, were around.

"It was the best childhood anyone could ever ask for," Jim reflected. "Perfect, actually, except for the year when I was eight, 1918, the year my sister Lucy was six and a terrible epidemic hit the country and our home. Influenza. It took my sister's life."

Shocked, Bill reached out and placed his hand on Jim's slumped shoulder. "I do remember that terrible time. I was serving in the army in France, but yes, I remember it very well. In fact, if I'm correct, it killed more people than the war itself. It was called the greatest medical holocaust in history. Oh, Jim, I am so sorry. That must have been so difficult for you and your family. I can't imagine losing a sister—and at such a young age."

At that delicate moment, the porch door opened and Peanut stepped out. She looked tired, and Bill detected fear.

"Hi," she said in a gentle whisper. "Is anyone else here?"

"No, just me and Mr. Walling. Are you feeling better?" Jim stood, and wiping away a tear, he gently guided her to one of the rocking chairs. "Here. Sit. I was just telling Mr. Walling about my family. About Lucy."

"Oh. I'm sorry to interrupt."

"No, no. Actually there is kind of a good end to the story that I hadn't gotten to yet."

Smiling, Jim took Peanut's hand in his as Bill sat patiently, wondering why Jim had opened up so much to him. We all need someone to talk to, to lean on, Bill thought, and he seemed to be in the right place at the right time for Jim. But something was also going on with Peanut. Should he ask? Should he excuse himself and join the girls on the beach? He was, after all, on vacation and clearly in no position to get involved in the lives of these two young people. Or should he just sit quietly and wait out this pending drama? It was another awkward moment.

Before Bill had the chance to excuse himself, Jim continued with his story.

"When Lucy died we were all devastated, but Mom and Dad saw to it that our lives went on as normally as possible. Lucy died in the fall, and returning to the beach the following summer was almost unbearable. No one here knew what had happened, so we had to tell everyone—it was like playing a broken record, and each time we told the story it got harder. We actually left and went home to Portland early that summer—it was just too much, especially for my mother.

"The next summer was better, and Mom let me take a job at the Jordan horse farm—the one you see across the river from the beach." Jim pointed to the left, where sprawling fields surrounded a large barn with fencing that extended in all directions. The silhouettes of horses could be seen in the fields.

Bill knew that his girls loved horses and wondered if they might go over to the farm during their stay.

"It's where I met Peanut."

"The horse farm?"

"Yes, it belongs to her uncle, the nicest man around. He often entertained Peanut when she was very young and her parents were too busy with their farming to keep an eye on her. When she grew up, oh, I'd say when she was about five or six, Peanut would find her way to the farm on her own and hang out with all of us and the horses. Her house is a short walk from the farm, and her parents were so busy, I don't think they even knew she was gone. It was all very safe—all family—and her cousins always kept a good eye on her."

Bill looked over at Peanut, who seemed to be just staring out at the point—at her house. A breeze had picked up, and as she adjusted the blanket over her shoulders, Bill caught a glimpse at what appeared to be a large bruise on her arm. Should he say something? Try again to excuse himself?

Giggles were suddenly heard and got louder as Annie and Janey appeared over the rocks. Phew. A welcome interruption. Bill stood and greeted his daughters as they bounded up the stairs to the porch, laden with their beach bounty.

"Pa! Look what we found!" Piles of shells fell onto the porch in bundles of wet, slimy seaweed. A few fairly large light-pink pieces stood out. "Look at these," Annie exclaimed. "Must be from some kind of sea monster!"

Laughing, Jim leaned over. "Actually, Annie, these are cooked lobster shells. Someone must have had a lobster bake on the beach last night."

"But shouldn't they go in the trash?" Annie was genuinely concerned.

"Not necessarily. The lobsters came from the sea, and the sea will wash away the shells with the next high tide. A natural cleaning lady."

Satisfied, Annie took her leave from the porch in search of something to drink. Bill excused himself and followed with Janey in tow. "Jim, I need to tend to the girls, but if you need me, we'll just be inside. Thank you for sharing your story."

"I'm sorry I let out so much, Mr. Walling. We barely know each other, but I really did need someone to talk to. Thank you for listening." With that, Jim gently led Peanut from the porch and back up to his room.

PEANUT

"So whhheeere the helllll were you yessssterrday? With that ciiity boy agaaaaain?"

His voice shook the dark room as Peanut crawled deeper under her covers. He scared her, and it was happening more and more. He was drunk—she could tell by the tone of his voice, the slur of his words, and the smell.

"Get out from that bed! You hear me?"

What time was it? She had been sound asleep and only faint moonlight graced the walls of her little room. Was it safe to get out of bed? What was her father going to do? She was alone with him—there was no one within earshot. What if he hurt her?

As these thoughts swam through her head, Peanut felt his strong grip on her arm dragging her to the floor.

"Dad! Please! Stop! You're hurting me!"

"You! Get up! I need to talk to you!"

Everything was a blur as fear took over and Peanut stood to face her father. He held her arms tightly, his eyes burning with anger.

"I have to go away for a few days," he said.

She could barely make out his words as he stumbled back a couple of steps and leaned against the wall.

"OK," she said hesitantly. "That's fine. I'll take care of things around here. When will you be back?"

"No idea. None of your business anyway. You just watch yourself, or when I get back I'll get you *good*!"

Abruptly, shakily, her father left the room and slammed the door behind him. She heard his heavy steps as he descended the stairs, then the crash of a door. He was gone. Drunk, angry, gone.

Terrified, Peanut returned to the safety of her bed, trembling as she considered what had just happened. He had been angry before—he didn't like her leaving the property as she had that afternoon. He didn't like Jim, and he knew that Jim was who she went to whenever she could get away, and Jim was one of *them*—a city boy, a summer person, one of those rich kids whose parents had taken over the old Higgins farm and destroyed the old way of life around here. He had told her as much many times. And he had been drunk before—regularly—although, at the time, she did know that alcohol was illegal. But he had never grabbed her before, never left before, and now she was scared—*really* scared. She could go to her uncle, but that would mean admitting her fear. Everyone would think that she had done something wrong; no one would believe her or help her. She would just have to give in and hope it would all go away.

But thinking more clearly, there was one thing that she *could* do.

That past winter, Peanut had figured out how to get into the tower. Although her father had locked it up tight after her mother's death, she saw him go in there now and then, usually at night when he thought she was asleep. One day, her curiosity took over. It was a cold, snowy winter day, and her father had been called to help over at the horse farm, where part of the barn roof had collapsed under the weight of the snow. She knew he would be gone most of the day, and, having completed her chores, she decided to try to get into the tower. The double door was heavily padlocked, and there was only a small window high up on the first floor. The second floor also had only one small window, but the top floor had three large windows on each side. That was her way in, if any of the windows were unlocked, but it had to be at least twenty-five feet up. She had to be careful not to leave footprints in the snow around the tower, so she stood in the dooryard for a long time pondering her options.

Looking up and around, occasionally glancing hopefully at Hobbs to see if he had any great ideas, Peanut's eyes landed on the apple tree next to the tower. Her favorite climbing tree as a child, it was close enough so that some of its branches, now weighted with snow, were actually touching the side of the tower, and a bank of snow had blown against that north side high enough for her to try out her climbing skills. She was strong and agile—always had been—and this would be the true test of her determination.

On the porch of the house was a small wooden bench, light enough for Peanut to drag through the snow and onto the embankment by the apple tree. Setting it on end created a stairway of sorts, and climbing it put her just a couple of feet from the tree's highest branches. It was an old, sturdy tree, and the branches proved strong enough to bear her weight as she ascended and found herself close enough to grab the lower sill of one of the windows. Hobbs barked as he watched her carefully position herself so that she could push the window open. First wiping the snow from the sill, Peanut could only hope that the window wasn't locked. Being so high up, there was a good chance that none of the windows had locks on them. And she was right! The window opened just enough for Peanut to squeeze her small frame through.

Hobbs continued to bark, but was soon assured of Peanut's safety and stopped at her command. Good dog! The midday winter sun reflecting off the snow provided sufficient light for Peanut to closely inspect the contents of the small, square room inside this mysterious tower her father had kept secret her entire life. Tool benches lined the four walls, each covered with an assortment of equipment that meant nothing to her. There were lanterns in two of the windows. She peered out. One of the windows faced the ocean; the other faced the beach. Wires twisted about, and she realized that these were electrical lanterns, ones that could be controlled by a switch and a button. They didn't even have anything this modern in the house!

On one wall, Peanut spotted a chart with letters of the alphabet each followed by a series of dots and dashes. She knew how to read—she was fifteen, after all, and quite good in school. Plus, Jim often read to her—poems, mostly—and she would follow along picking up new words as he went.

It wasn't long before Peanut was trying out the lanterns herself. They worked, and by using the button, she could copy the dash-dot series to make words. Was that what this was for? To send words with light? Did her father use this to send messages to someone? Why? Where? Who? Well, this was something Peanut was determined to find out.

She must have spent an hour or more poking around in the tower. Stairs led to the ground floor; the second floor was but a loft filled mostly with hay. It was dark down below with only the two small windows, both of which were very high up and let in little light. The ground floor was nothing but dirt covered largely by wooden crates stacked three and four high. There must have been at least fifty of them.

With a metal crowbar she found hanging on the wall, Peanut carefully opened one of the crates. Inside, a dozen or so brown glass bottles were packed tightly together. Lifting one out, Peanut immediately realized what she had discovered—whiskey! Lots of whiskey!

Somewhat scared and nervous at this point, Peanut quickly replaced the bottle, secured the crate, and was ready to leave her discovery when she spotted keys hanging on a nail by the double door to the outside. Inspecting them closely, she realized that the three keys were all the same. Barely thinking, she grabbed one and placed it in her coat pocket before dashing up the stairs and out the window. Phew! Hobbs was still there, and there was no sign of anyone else around.

She returned the bench to the porch and grabbed her wooden sled. She would need to cover any tracks or other signs of her clandestine activity. Turning the snow bank against the tower into a sledding hill, she climbed up and slid down over and over again until the last bit of energy left her. Collapsing in a pile, wet with snow, Hobbs licking her face, fingering the key in her pocket, Peanut called it a day and went inside to heat up some soup.

That had been five months ago. This was now. Peanut was hurt—her father had left quite a bruise on her arm. She was scared. She was alone for now, and who knew what her father would do when he returned. And when *would* he return? Where had he gone?

MONDAY, JULY 18, 1932, 5:30 P.M.

*B*ill and the girls had spent the afternoon on the beach wandering aimlessly as the incoming tide pushed them closer and closer to shore. High tide peaked around 4:00 but left enough sand for them to continue their stay, nestling their blankets in the crevices of the rocky embankment. The waves were small and gentle. A soft breeze kicked up, pushing the warm air in their already perspiring faces. The Maine waters rarely reached 65 degrees, but temptation won out.

"I heard that if you put your wrists in the water, it helps you adjust to the cold—it's supposed to make it easier to go in all the way." With skepticism in his voice, Bill coaxed the girls knee-deep into the ocean swells. One by one, laughing uncontrollably, Annie, Janey, and Bill quickly submerged themselves in the cold water and bounced back up in total glee. After a few dunks each, they all agreed that it was mission accomplished.

Showers at the inn were outside, and although they were cold water only, they were refreshing and cleansed the sand and salt away. After dressing, Bill, Janey, and Annie hung their suits and towels on the line behind the inn and found their way to the porch, where the late-afternoon sun beat warmth upon them. Bill had grabbed the backgammon board. Annie and Janey had found some lemonade and cookies to hold them over until dinner. What Bill had really had in mind for this beach vacation had truly set in.

"Jim!" Annie exclaimed from one end of the porch.

Turning, Bill watched Jim approach from the dirt path below. He looked better. More relaxed.

"Come sit, Jim. Janey has me in suspense. I just taught her this game yesterday, and she's really taken to it. Are you familiar with backgammon?"

Jim sat and peered at the board between Bill and Janey. No, he didn't know this one.

"I'm winning!" Janey said proudly. "And Pa—he's the New York champ. He even wrote a book on how to play. See."

Sure enough. The book in front of Jim had William H. Walling as its author. He looked up with surprise and awe.

"I've never met an author before," Jim said with a smile.

"Well, it's just a passion I have, and it led to this little guide. Nothing too spectacular, but I must admit, it is something I'm quite proud of.

"So, things better for you this afternoon?" Bill continued cautiously.

"Yeah. Peanut has gone to her uncle's for a few days—the one who owns the horse farm over on the point where I used to work. He's a nice man and has always had a fondness for her—his niece."

"Well, that's good." What else could Bill say? He really didn't know what was going on, but surely things were not right.

"Her father has gone away for a bit. Work. Should be home before too long—Wednesday or Thursday? Maybe Friday? I'm not sure."

"*Wednesday!*" A thrill in Annie's voice made all heads turn. "That's my birthday!"

"Yes, dearie, it certainly is." Bill confirmed with a huge smile. "We'll have to do something to celebrate, don't you think?"

"How old will you be?" said Jim, embracing her excitement.

"Seven. Right, Pa?"

"Seven it will be. My lucky number for my special girl! And we'll make sure it's a special day. But right now, I think your sister and I should finish this game so we can get ready for dinner. Jim, would you like to join us?"

"Well, sure. That would be nice. I'm going to head upstairs, but I'll meet you back down here in a few minutes. Thanks for including me."

Jim excused himself as Bill and Janey finished the game—Janey winning for the first time—and Annie rolled marbles across the porch.

EARLY MAY 2017

*D*ad will be moving to assisted living in two weeks. It brings mixed feelings. I will be relieved that he gets more care and attention, which he clearly needs, but it is also the end of this stage in his life—and in mine. He is old. I am getting older. He can no longer live independently. I have gotten used to the idea that Mom needs to be where she is. Now it's Dad. And to leave this beautiful apartment with its views of the ocean and so many memories of the past dozen years. What emotions am I feeling? Actually, I think I'm operating on automatic, doing what needs to be done while keeping emotions aside as best I can.

My youngest son is coming home from Colorado for a brief visit. He's a great kid and loves his grandparents. Top priority for both of us is time for him with Mom and Dad. When I moved to Scarborough, one of the first things I did was have a ramp made for the doorway into the house so I could get Mom inside in her wheelchair. She has only visited three times in over a year, but each time has warmed my heart. She likes my little house. Dad does as well. They are happy to have me close by.

My son is turning 26 at the end of the month. Birthdays have always been very special occasions in my family, surpassed only by Christmas. I can remember my childhood birthdays well, but have always cherished my shared birthdays with Mom the most as they are just five days apart.

I don't know if this will be the last time my son sees his grandmother, and maybe even his grandfather, but I will treat it as if it is. Despite the relative chaos of moving Dad and emptying the apartment in the next two weeks, I take time to arrange for transportation for Mom and Dad to come to my house for lunch while my son is here. We'll have a birthday party for him! Why not?

The visit goes well, at least the best that can be expected. Mom and Dad quietly enjoy their time together—time they so rarely get anymore, awake. We enjoy sandwiches and a small birthday cake. We sing. We go through the motions as best we can. I can see a rainbow of emotions in my son's eyes and can feel them in his heart. He has lost both grandparents on his father's side, both of whom he was very close to. Now this. Knowing but not knowing. Smiling but not smiling. Only one thing is certain: we all share the deepest love for each other and carry the burden of eventuality in our souls.

Dad is typically quiet, but at one point, Mom seems eager to talk. Her eyes almost speak for her. I respond.

"Hey, Mom. You have always loved birthdays, haven't you?" She returns a smile. "I can remember mine—summer, Quogue, under Ma's pear trees, by the rose garden with lots of friends."

"Balloons." I hear a whisper.

"Yes, Mom. We always had balloons. Most of them ended up flying away, though."

"Balloons in the tree."

I reflect as she tries to describe her memories.

"It was fun. Thanks for always giving me the best birthday." I turn to see her give in to her leaning right side. Her eyes looking weary. Time to go back. It has been almost an hour—not bad. This will be Mom's (and Dad's, as it turns out) last visit to my house.

Tired but alert, she gets settled back in her room with the help of the nurses. My son gives her a gentle kiss on the forehead. "See you soon, Annie. I love you."

"Love you, too."

WEDNESDAY, JULY 20, 1932

Annie's seventh birthday had arrived!

On Monday night, after a nice dinner, Jim had joined Bill on the porch while the girls retreated to their room early. The summer sun and surf had begun to take their toll, and vacation time meant cuddling in bed as much as anything else.

"Hey, Mr. Walling."

"Please call me Bill. I asked that of you before; now I demand it," Bill chuckled. "Things better with Peanut now that she's at her uncle's?"

"Oh, yes, she will be fine there. I know you saw how upset she was this morning. It's her father."

"Jim, you don't need to tell me anything if you don't want to."

"I know, but it does help to let it out. You see, Peanut is like a sister to me. Even more. When Lucy died, Peanut was just a baby, but as she grew up, we became really good friends—especially after her mother died four years ago. In a way, we were both dealing with the same thing. Loss. Loss of someone we loved, who loved us. It drew me and Peanut very close. Her father is hard on her. She's scared of him, and it's just getting worse. He's been drinking a lot—may be a bootlegger for all I know. Last night, he actually hurt Peanut in one of his rages. All she wanted to do was escape. That's why I brought her here this morning, and now she's at her uncle's. I'm not sure what else I can do."

Pondering Jim's words, Bill could only count his blessings. Yes, maybe his marriage hadn't lasted, maybe he only saw his girls a few times a year, but they were safe and well cared for. He didn't have to worry about them, whether they were with him or not.

"You know, Bill. I have an idea. Something that might help Peanut but would also be fun for all of us."

"And what might that be?"

"Why don't Peanut and I give Annie a birthday party on Wednesday? I never celebrated Lucy's seventh birthday, so why not Annie's? And it would be fun—a distraction for Peanut. She'd love it!"

"It's awfully nice of you to propose that. I'm not a great party planner, especially for a little girl, so I guess, if you have the inclination, it could work out for all of us. I had been struggling with ideas, and I know Annie will be—actually *is*—hoping for something."

With that, the plans were laid. On Tuesday, Jim brought Peanut to the inn, and together they made all the arrangements: the inn would bake a cake and lend them their croquet set. A trip to The Pavilion resulted in a bag of balloons, a ball of ribbon, the makings for PB & J's, some chips and pickles, and a few party favors (Bill had said that money was no object). Peanut busied herself collecting shells on the beach, and Bill kept the girls occupied for the day by taking them on a scenic trolley ride along the coast.

When Jim returned Peanut to her uncle's, invitations to the party were extended to her cousins and their friends. The more the merrier. Finally, Jim tracked down Al, the local lobsterman who kept his traps and dory at a small dock on the river, and he agreed to shuttle Bill and the girls over in his boat Wednesday at noon. The party would be at Peanut's house and a total surprise. Any chance of her father returning was unlikely, and her uncle had said unconditionally that he would handle that part of it if necessary.

Wednesday morning, a few clouds filtered the rising sun, but not enough to avoid waking anyone sleeping in an east-facing room with no curtains. "Hey, Annie," Janey whispered. "Happy birthday!"

Annie lifted her head, groggy but unable to hold back her excitement. It was her special day! She was seven! *I hope Pa remembers*—the first thought to pop into her head. She was usually in Cooperstown with her mother and her many cousins on her birthday, and no one ever forgot! *Well*, she thought, *if he did forget, I won't say anything. I don't want him to feel bad.*

At that very moment, the door to her room opened to reveal Bill holding a bouquet of wild beach roses. "It's all I could find for *my* birthday girl."

A huge smile appeared from under the sheets as Bill stood proudly in the doorway.

"Pa! You remembered!"

Before he knew it, two arms were wrapped around his thighs. The best hug he'd had in a long time.

"Well, you deserve nothing less, Annie dear. And if we can get your sister moving, we have a big day ahead."

Janey jumped from her bed with a small bag in her hands and handed it to her sister. "It's for you. Nothing much, but it's the thought that counts. Pa probably will make you wait until later, but I hope you like these."

It was a collection of penny candy—fireballs, Twizzlers, Mary Janes, gummi bears, taffy, candy buttons, Tootsie Rolls— any seven-year-old's dream.

66

"Ohhhhh, Janey! We never get to eat candy like this at home! Thank you! I promise I'll share some."

It was a simple but special start to a perfect birthday, a birthday that Annie would never forget.

The day was a bit cooler than it had been, with a light breeze coming off the ocean. As they ate breakfast shielded by the windows of the dining room, Bill, Janey, and Annie watched the outgoing tide expose more and more beach. It was different every day—fascinating to watch the rhythm of nature playing its tune before their very eyes. And although forever changing, the changes were subtle, much like the changes taking place in their own lives. With the girls engrossed in their blueberry pancakes, Bill contemplated the constancy of the natural world around him. The breeze, the laughing gulls, the rolling waves, the clouds sailing gracefully above to places unknown. Steady. Intentional. Simple, but complex. Beautiful. Beyond. So much greater than himself, but there at his fingertips, giving him a true sense of wonder, peace, and gratitude. Gratitude for his tiny place in this great universe and the two young women under his wings—at least for now.

Breakfast was over. Low tide was at noon, and Al would be waiting. It would take them a good thirty minutes to walk to the river. It was time for the festivities to begin.

"I have some plans for us today, dearies," Bill announced. "But we won't be on the beach, so go and put on some play clothes, and wear some sturdy shoes."

"Sure, Pa." The girls looked at him with suspicious excitement. "Can you tell us what we're doing? Where we're going?"

"Not if you like surprises!"

As the girls ran up the stairs to their room, Jim quietly approached from the kitchen doorway. "We all set?"

"Seems that way. We'll be at the river at noon."

"Perfect. Just follow the beach road to the end, cross onto the beach toward the river. Al will be there. Peanut and I will be on the other side. You'll see us—it's only a few feet, no more than fifty across at low tide. Peanut is so excited to do this—it has really helped her mood. Kept her mind off things. And no sign of her father."

"Can't wait. You better run before the girls see you. Oh, and don't forget to let me know what I owe you for everything. Thanks so much. Annie's going to be thrilled! Janey, too, I hope."

Bill looked at his pocket watch and realized he had an hour to spare. He pondered his options for keeping the girls preoccupied. He had told them to dress, so the beach was out. A walk to The Pavilion might work, but he didn't really need anything, and they certainly didn't need sweets before the party. A ride in the roadster with the top down might work—a tour to the south, maybe. He had heard that nearby Prouts Neck was pretty spectacular with the huge, historic Checkley Hotel and stately seaside homes overlooking the rocky cliffs. And so it was.

No sooner had they arrived back at the inn when Bill found himself the target of an excited birthday girl. They weren't even out of the car yet.

"Pa, what are we going to do for lunch?" the always hungry Annie inquired. "You said there was a surprise for me. Will it be coming soon? When can we celebrate my birthday? We are, aren't we?"

So many questions. So much anticipation. So much adorable energy. Bill just observed, listened, and chuckled.

"Well, I suppose we could head off now," Bill responded as they emerged from the car.

"Head off? Again? Where to this time?" Janey asked quietly and, not surprisingly, with a hint of irritation. She wasn't so sure she could take all this attention being given to her sister.

Bill did a final check of the girls—play clothes, comfortable shoes, nothing to carry, hair pinned back. Seemed they were ready to go. Eleven-thirty a.m.—just enough time to take a casual walk past the cottages to the beach where it met the river. Grabbing a hand in each of his, they were off.

As planned, they were greeted by Al and his twelve-foot dory at the edge of the river. "Needin' a ride?" he bellowed with a grin as they approached.

Al was a solid man. Most likely in his early sixties, Bill thought. Definitely a fisherman by the looks of his waders and boots. His oilskin hat, not to say anything of his calloused hands, showed the wear of his years on the water. Apparently, he had been lobstering this area for forty years and had set close to a hundred traps as far as eight miles away from the river. He lived here at Higgins Beach with his wife and was known for the beautiful duck decoys that he made and sold to the tourists. Bill thought he might have to purchase one before vacation was over.

"Nice to meet you, Al. Jim has told us quite a bit about you. Bill Walling," he extended his hand. "These are my daughters, Janey and Annie. Girls—" Bill waited as they quietly approached with expressions of wonder and curiosity.

"Are we going in that boat?" Annie blurted out.

"Yep," said Al. "Go ahead 'n climb in. Your friend Jim was askin' me if I could take you, your sistah and your fathah 'cross the river to the farm beyond the-ah," he said, pointing behind himself to the hillside fields across the river. Al reached for Annie's hand to help her into the boat, but it didn't happen.

"Wait! What are those?" a typically distracted Annie exclaimed as she approached a pile of lobster traps stacked on the sand.

"Oh, those're traps to catch lobstahs. See, he-ah," Al pointed to the slatted wooden traps with their intricate rope webbing. "Do ya know how to catch a lobstah? Have ya ever eaten one?"

"Pa said we could have lobster while we're here, but we haven't tried it yet. Those traps go out in the ocean, right?"

"Well, yeah. I take the traps out in the boat, put some bait in 'em—usually dead fish—an' drop 'em into the sea on a long rope. They each got a brick in the-ah so they sink. At th'other end of the rope, I have a buoy so I can find 'em later and lift 'em back out."

Annie listened attentively. Al's strong Maine accent didn't seem to impress Annie one bit, though Janey stared at him in awe as she and Bill waited, eager to get going.

"The trap is kinda like a house. See heah? This is called the kitchen. It's where I put the bait. The lobstahs come in through one of these heah nets to get the bait, and once they're in, they can't get out."

"How many lobsters do you catch?"

"It depends. I can only handle a few traps at a time in the dory, so I make a numbah a trips out. On a good day, I might put out fifty or sixty traps and bring home more'n a hundred lobstahs. But that's a good day. Sometimes the lobstahs're too small to keep. Can't keep any female lobstahs with eggs, ya know. Some days, I get just enough to feed me and my wife."

"Annie," Bill interrupted, "we have a schedule to keep."

"Just climb in right heah, girls, but be careful—the mud can be slipp'ry an' those mussel shells can cut your feet bad if ya shoes come off." Al led Annie back to the boat. "Both of ya can sit on this seat right heah. Bill, help me give 'er a push, then jump on in. It's low tide, just about to turn, so the watah's pretty slack. Should have ya on the other side in no time. And sorry 'bout your shoes, the mud. Looks like you may need ta wash 'em later."

"We're going across!" Annie exclaimed with absolutely no concern about her muddy shoes. "Oh, look, Pa! There's Jim on the other side! And Peanut's with him—with Hobbs!"

Once everyone was situated, Al took long, powerful strokes with the two wooden oars, propelling the dory forward. A couple of eider ducks swam in the boat's gentle wake. Seagulls on the rocky shore ahead flew gracefully away as the dory approached.

"Hey, Annie! Janey! Bill! Welcome to Jordan Farm!" Jim's greeting brought screams and laughter as Al assisted everyone out of the boat and onto the shore.

"Happy birthday, Annie! We have a few surprises planned for you. Just follow me."

"Hi, Annie," Peanut said with a warm smile as she walked over to greet everyone. "Happy birthday."

Bill looked on. Peanut seemed OK but very quiet as they began the walk up to the farm. She stayed close to Jim, with Hobbs trailing at her feet, as Bill, Annie, and Janey followed, taking in the surrounding farmland, the fenced field with grazing horses, and the beautiful barn atop the hill awaiting their arrival.

"Have you ever ridden a horse, Annie?" Jim asked, knowing that she loved horses but not whether she'd ever ridden one.

"Me? No! I live in the city, remember? The only horses we have there belong to the police."

"Well, I'd like to introduce you to Rhubarb. Come with me."

As Annie followed Jim into the barn, Peanut guided Bill and Janey to a small wagon hitched up and ready to go. "Jim is going to ride with Annie, and I'll take the two of you in the wagon."

"Where are we going?" Janey was clearly a bit anxious, not having been privy to what her father had been arranging with Jim to celebrate Annie's birthday. Obviously, they wanted this to be a very special day. Too bad it was all for her sister, not her. Oh well, she would make the most of it even if she wasn't the one in the spotlight.

"We're headed up the road to my house. You've seen it from the beach, right? The one at the end of the point."

"Oh, yeah. Annie pointed it out to me. The one with the tower. I guess Jim told her you lived there. Nice spot."

"Well, hop on in. I see Jim has Annie on Rhubarb, so I guess we're ready to go."

It was a short but lovely ride just above the rocky shoreline, through fields and patches of pine forest. The view of Higgins Beach was spectacular!

"Janey dear." Bill put his arm around his older daughter, making sure she felt as special as her sister. "This is quite something, isn't it?"

Feeling a bit more relaxed and confident, Janey had question after question for Peanut. "How old are you? Do you have any brothers or sisters? Have you always lived here? Where are your mother and father? How old is your dog? Where do you go to school?"

Aware of Peanut's tender state, Bill tried to intercede, but Peanut took it all with grace and responded cheerfully to Janey's inquiries.

"I'm fifteen and have lived here all my life. My mother died four years ago. I live with my father, but he's away right now. My uncles own all this farmland—they take care of me when my father's away. You met my father at the farmers' market last Saturday. Remember?"

"I guess so. I was so busy looking at all the people and food, I must have forgotten that you were there."

"Well, we've planned a birthday party for Annie at my house. It was your father's idea—I guess Jim's, too. Anyway, we've invited some of my cousins and have some food and games. It should be fun."

As they rounded the last turn, Janey lit up in awe. Balloons, dozens of them in all colors of the rainbow, hung from the big apple tree next to the house. A group of children ran in circles chasing a kick ball. Tables of food were set out in the yard. Janey looked back for Annie and Jim, who were still out of sight beyond the bend. Boy, was her sister going to be surprised!

And was she ever! Guided by Jim, Annie brought Rhubarb up to the fencepost by the house, dismounted, and stood in total disbelief as Jim secured the horses and led her over to meet the other children. A chorus of "Happy Birthday" broke out with even Hobbs joining in with howls of delight. The party had begun.

It was a day to remember. In between munching on sandwiches, chips, and pickles, Jim and Peanut oversaw three-legged races, games of pin the tail on the donkey, and a craft table where the children made necklaces of clam shells that Peanut had gathered from the beach. Bill and the uncles played a game of croquet and then retreated to the shade of the balloon-covered apple tree to take in the delight surrounding them. The afternoon ended with the cutting of a beautiful birthday cake that Jim had secured from the inn.

"Well, Jim. This could not have been better," Bill sighed as the festivities came to a close. "For everyone."

"You're right." Jim acknowledged. "It was a perfect way to lift Peanut's spirits. And Annie sure had the time of her life. Was Janey OK? She seemed a bit shy."

"Oh, she's probably just jealous. You know. Sisters can be a bit competitive. Sometimes it's hard to share all the attention."

"I can relate." Jim's head dropped a bit, and Bill remembered that he had lost one of his sisters.

"Sorry. I didn't mean to ruin things for you. You did such a great job today. I can't thank you enough."

"It was my pleasure. I'm OK—just miss my sister every now and then. "

"Should we clean up this mess?" Bill glanced around at popped balloons, stacks of plates, scattered croquet balls, little piles of sand and clam shells, evidence of a great time had by all.

"Oh, don't worry about it. My cousins said they would take care of everything. Peanut and I will take you back to the inn.

We'll let Annie ride Rhubarb again to the barn and then take the wagon around."

Bill smiled. "You have it all figured out, don't you?"

MID-MAY 2017

*M*ay 16, 2017. Moving day.

I really would have preferred to spend more time tending my little garden. Despite the cool, gray, damp weather we've been having, all of my bulbs are up, the nightshade at the end of the driveway is in full bloom, and it's time to put in a few veggies.

It took coordination and planning to get to this day. A *lot* of coordination and planning—and an inner strength that, re-markably, I seemed to be able to rustle up at times like this. It is now fully deployed as I await my siblings and the movers as scheduled. Dad is sitting quietly in his chair at the dining room table, jacket on, trusting me that all will be OK. He is going to go out to lunch with my brother while the move takes place. I've given him enough of his own cash to pay for lunch, as I know this is very important to him. When he returns, he will be in his new home, a two-room apartment in assisted living overlooking the parking lot, one floor above the health center where Mom is.

Mom's nurses are preparing her for lunch—a perfect time to take her bureau, mirror, side table, two upholstered chairs, and a few paintings (of her dogs!) to her room. They need to go somewhere, and maybe a little bit of home will make her room feel less like she's in a hospital—if not for her, at least for me. My sister oversees this while I direct the movers with everything else for the new apartment.

By the time Dad returns from lunch, his assisted living apartment is ready and waiting. It is very emotional for me: I want it to feel like home. I want him to be comfortable, and I want to help him accept this next stage in his life. I've planned the layout so that it looks and feels as close to what he left as possible. I am holding back tears as he walks through the door and is greeted by a miniature version of the apartment he and Mom called home for twelve years. He smiles as he heads for "his" chair, its back to the window (as he prefers), lamp overhead, small table at its side, footrest in place, facing out to the familiar dining room table, the TV and bench with his newspaper and magazines, a tall bookshelf of photo albums, and the two table lamps with shades depicting images of the front and back of our old house in Connecticut. He breaks just a small smile, but for Dad, that says it all. I think it's going to be alright.

Phew! Mom and Dad are now a bit closer—just a quick elevator ride—and maybe I can get them together with each other more often, and with me. Yes, we'll have lunch in the assisted living dining room. I know it will be an early lunch hour for Dad, but there are some things he's just going to have to adjust to.

Three days after Dad's move, I bring Mom up for lunch. It's a bright, sunny day. The assisted living dining room is quite nice, smaller than the health center's and more like the main dining room, with tables featuring linens, centerpieces, and silver. We settle in at a table for four by the window, my dog at my feet. No one seems to care that she's in here (unlike downstairs), and I feel complete.

Lunch is nice. Mom and Dad are quiet. No one eats very much, but we spend nearly an hour together and share an occasional smile. I really hope we can do this regularly. It's good for all of us.

Wishful thinking! Just four days later—one week after Dad's move—I get the dreaded call: "We've taken him in."

Am I supposed to know what that means? It doesn't sound good; I could use a little more specific information.

"Taken him in? Do you mean that he's gone to the emergency room?"

Of course, yes, he has gone to the emergency room complaining of pain, acting confused and delusional, clear signs of another urinary tract infection.

After over eight hours in the emergency room, I bring Dad back at, of all hours, 11 p.m. I guess the hospital does everything it can to avoid admitting a patient and keeping them overnight. This is awful! Dad is still confused, still in pain and now with a catheter, and the night nurses in assisted living are overwhelmed, forcing their way through the process of cleaning him up and settling him back in bed.

I'm beginning to lose it. I don't know if I can find the strength to take much more of this—emptying the apartment, trying to see Mom as much as I can (now she is failing faster than she has in a long time), helping Dad settle into his new environment, Dad sick, the unexpected visit to the emergency room, new nurses in assisted living whom I don't know, who Dad doesn't know, and who don't seem to know much about us. Of course, he is new to them. I am new to them. He has arrived with problems. No one is prepared, including me.

Mom. I need my mom. She isn't eating very well these days. In fact, a special nurse/therapist has been assigned to help her with her meals. Today, rather than sit in the busy dining room, I join Mom at a small table in the hallway. Waiting for her lunch to arrive, I lose it and tears stream down my face. I am literally sobbing. "Sorry, Mom. It's just so hard. Dad is not well. I am tired. I feel so alone." Her hand reaches out. I look in amazement and take it in mine. We look each other in the eye as she holds my hand. My tears continue as she works on a smile. I feel her love.

76

She says nothing, but she doesn't have to. She is there for me. She always has been and she is now.

PEANUT & JIM

"*I* just don't know what to do. I can't live here anymore. I have to get out. He's going to really hurt me and I'm scared. Oh, Jim. Jim. Can you help me? You're the only one that can help me."

Trembling, Peanut collapsed in Jim's arms, sobbing, begging, near hysterics. The smell of hay permeated the barn as they curled up in an empty stall trying to figure out what to do next. The day had been a huge success. Everyone, especially Annie, had loved the birthday party. It had taken Peanut's mind off her father and the pain that he had inflicted on her. But now it was over, and it was time for Jim to leave her at her uncle's not knowing when her father would return and, when he did return, not knowing what he would do.

"I'm scared, too, Peanut. For you. You're like a sister to me—more than a sister. I know your father. I've seen how he's changed since your mother died. He's an angry man. He drinks too much. And now it seems he's gotten himself involved in some messy business."

"He has. I told you about all the bottles of whiskey I found in the tower. And those lights we've been using to signal each other. He has those because I think he's smuggling alcohol—helping boats come ashore and stashing their liquor for them. He's some kind of middleman and I think it's getting him in trouble. But the worst of it is that he's started taking his problems out on me! He wants me gone! Out of his business—out of his life. I'm just a burden and a threat to him. I think he's actually scared of me now that I'm getting older and might figure out what he's up to. Well, I have figured out what he's up to, and I want no part of it!"

Jim had known this day would come. In one sense, he actually welcomed it. In another, it terrified him. He had a choice to make, one that had occupied his mind for a long time.

His family had moved to the Midwest. He was an adult, young, yes, but an adult. He had chosen an independent life remaining here in Maine. He had a good job. He had saved a fair amount of money. He felt that he had a head on his shoulders, but he also had a heart that he could not ignore. If he was honest with himself, he would admit that his motives were not necessarily admirable. He knew what he *wanted* to do. He was not sure of what he *should* do. He didn't want to hurt anyone. In reality, there was no one who would get hurt. He would talk to Peanut's uncle, explain his plan, make the promises he had been holding so close to his heart for so long—promises he planned to keep.

The dinner bell rang, a signal for Peanut to head into her uncle's house.

"I have to go." Tears still stood in Peanut's eyes as she looked longingly at Jim.

"Yes. Go on. You'll be fine. Go have some supper, and I'll head back to the inn. I don't think your father will be back anytime soon. I am working on a plan. I just need a day or so to figure a few things out. You'll be safe here with your uncle. I'll come by tomorrow to check on you."

"You have a plan? To help me?"

"Well, I've been thinking about you—about us—for a long time. It's one of the reasons I didn't move with my family. I want to help you.... No, I want to be with you. Forever."

"Oh, Jim." Peanut gazed into his eyes as he helped her to her feet and toward the barn door.

"Say nothing, Peanut. Please. I have a lot to work out, to think over. You just go ahead and I'll see you tomorrow. Here— this will explain," Jim assured her as he placed a folded piece of paper in her hand. "Just do what it says."

Peanut clutched the paper tightly, pulled away from Jim, and headed to the house. She trusted him. He would help her. Looking back, she watched him mount his bike and ride quickly down the dirt road toward Higgins Beach. It had been a good day and, if Jim was right, more good days were to come.

LATE MAY 2017

Dad is pretty much bedridden now, recuperating from his UTI and adjusting to having a catheter. He's comfortable, but this is clearly not what we bargained for. The nurses seem to be tending to his needs, but I don't think this is what they bargained for, either. They do get him up and out in his chair periodically. I hang pictures as a way of keeping busy, and hoping to bring him some enjoyment. His eyesight is almost gone, so I try to make fun out of describing the pictures, recalling memories and involving him in the process. He has a nice smile, and it helps me move along pretending that everything is OK.

Lunches with Mom continue, mostly in the hallway now, and it is nice to be able to suggest that we take a walk and go see Dad afterwards without having to go outside. She likes his new apartment, and I can take here there—unlike their old apartment, which had been her home, too—knowing that it won't bring up memories and cause undue stress.

I tell her that Dad has not been well, that he had to go to the emergency room.

"Why doesn't he just go to sleep?" she asks innocently.

"What? To sleep…forever? Is that what you mean?"

"Yes. He should just go to sleep."

"Mom, really. Do *you* want to 'just go to sleep'?"

"Of course not!"

"Well, I don't think he does, either." It feels good to laugh. It's fun to see that spark in Mom even if she is totally unaware of what she's saying. Is she, though?

My parents have never made a public display of their love and affection. I have very few memories of seeing them hug or even hold hands. I do remember taking the suggestion from a self-help book a few years ago of things to do to "enliven" your life. One was "Take a picture of your parents kissing." Well, that sounded like fun, so I gave it a try. It was hysterical! They actually didn't know what to do. It worked, but only after lots of encouragement—and of course, their dog was on Mom's lap getting most of the attention. My photo of them, all three, sits on my kitchen windowsill bringing a smile to my face every day.

Surprisingly, today I do get to see them hold hands. The day after Dad's visit to the emergency room, I take Mom up to see him. He's in bed but awake. I push her to the side of his bed.

"Hi, Chet." It's nice that, despite her accelerating dementia, Mom has not forgotten who we are.

Dad smiles and extends his hand out to her. I am almost in disbelief. She takes his hand. All I see is a very private, very loving moment that actually shocks me. I quietly back out of the room to let them have this time together alone. I feel like I am melting. I am witnessing a raw tenderness, a love so deep, a love that my parents have never exposed to me in this way before— and all in such a simple gesture.

Only a minute or two goes by before I sense Mom's restlessness. I step back into Dad's bedroom. Their hands have released.

"Ready to go, Mom?" She's already trying to push herself backward out of the room.

"OK. Dad, we'll see you later. Love you." I lean over and kiss his forehead.

JIM

Jim had prepared for this. He had known that the day would come when he would have to decide just how far he would go to ensure Peanut's safety, and to ensure that he would not lose her.

The note he had left with Peanut Wednesday evening was brief. They had talked about what they would do if this day arrived, so Jim knew he need not say more:

Pack. Tomorrow. Your uncle will know. Send a signal. Go to the cottage. I will come Friday morning—before dawn.

Thursday morning, Jim rose early hoping to avoid running into Bill, Janey, and Annie. He descended from his room to the inn's kitchen knowing he would find the owners busily preparing breakfast for the guests.

"Anything you need from the city today?" he asked hopefully of the innkeeper.

"Well, actually, now that you ask, we have an order of meat at the butcher's that I was heading in to pick up. Why? You going in today?"

"I thought I might. There a few things I need to tend to. I'd be happy to do errands for you."

"That would be a great help. Here," the innkeeper reached

into his pocket and handed Jim a set of keys, "why don't you take the car? You'll need it if you pick up the meat. Will save you time, too, with the trolley schedule as it is."

Just what Jim had hoped for, an easy way in and out of Portland to tend to his list of things to put in place in just one day.

He was determined to make this work. He had thought about his pending actions over and over again. He knew that in one sense it was wrong, but in another, it was right for both of them and would not hurt anyone. It would, in fact, save Peanut from a lot of harm and give them both a fresh start at a life together. Yes, it was a crime because Peanut was a minor. But, if they posed as brother and sister as planned, it should work. It had to work.

In just a few hours, Jim accomplished a lot. He closed his bank account, taking his savings in cash—enough to cover them until he figured out the next step in their journey. He released his keys to the room he had rented in the boardinghouse and managed to get his belongings into two duffels. He purchased two train tickets for the 8 a.m. car from Portland to Boston the following morning. Finally, he sent a telegram to the new owners of his family's Higgins Beach cottage at their winter home in Boston:

Coming tomorrow as planned. Using cottage tonight. Will secure.

Jim had become quite close to the young couple that had purchased the cottage two years before. Only a few years older than Jim, the husband was a partner in a very successful jewelry company that had been founded in 1840 by his great-grandfather and passed down through the family to his father, who now owned and managed the business. Originally dealing solely in diamonds at a time when most jewelers focused primarily on pearls, by the 1880s the company had two branches overseas and had expanded its line to include sapphires, rubies, emeralds and opals. Having weathered the Great Depression, Jim's friends enjoyed a well-endowed lifestyle in Boston and had chosen the southern coast of Maine for their summer retreats. They were expecting their first child in the fall and planned to take full advantage of the Higgins Beach cottage in future summers as their family grew. This particular season, they had visited only periodically, leaving the cottage for Jim to keep an eye on. He didn't use it, but tonight he would, and he let them know to keep his conscious clear. Committing one crime was enough; he needed to be aboveboard about the rest of his actions.

There were only two more tasks at hand, neither of which would be as easy as those first few. First, he needed to talk to Peanut's uncle to let him know of their plans. Her uncle was a fair man, a kind man, and he was well aware of the threat facing his niece. Jim hoped he would understand and provide cover. It was a risk, but Jim felt fairly confident that it would work out.

Before returning to the inn, Jim drove to the Jordan farm hoping to find Peanut's uncle in the barn putting the horses to rest for the night. Peanut would most likely be inside helping prepare dinner. His timing seemed just right. He didn't need to see Peanut—she knew what to do. He just needed to tell her uncle that the time had come.

"Peanut will be leaving tonight," he said, his heart pounding in his chest. "She's not safe here and we have a plan. I promise I will keep her safe."

"I know. There's nothing I can do. My brother…" Peanut's uncle sounded defeated. "He's not right. He's gotten himself into some kind of trouble. I didn't have to worry about Peanut when her mother was alive. But now…now, I just can't…I can't take care of her. I have my own children, I have the farm; I'm sorry. I know you will make sure she is all right."

"Yes, I will. And we won't be coming back, you know?"

"I do—and I think that's probably for the best. I hope you two can find somewhere safe where she can grow to be the wonderful person I know she *can* be. She's a good girl. Always has been. She deserves more—more than anyone here can give her. And she deserves to escape from the fear that she's been living in."

What more needed to be said? Jim reached out his hand and looked Peanut's uncle directly in the eye. "Thank you for your trust."

With those final words and a firm handshake, he left to find the last person he needed to speak to before his plan took hold.

PEANUT

Dinner with her aunt, uncle, and three cousins was relaxed, and for Peanut, surprisingly normal. She helped clear the dishes as usual and then headed out for a short walk with Hobbs. The sun would not set for another two hours, so she had plenty of time. She felt somewhat exhilarated but also very anxious about what lay ahead. She knew she had little choice. She knew Jim would take care of her.

She returned to her uncle's to say goodbye. Her cousins were upstairs getting ready for bed so it was quick. She started out toward her own house for the last time with Hobbs at her side.

"You can leave Hobbs with us," her uncle's voice came from behind her. "He'll be fine. You know we love him and will take good care of him for you."

Peanut turned slowly. Did she see tears welling in her uncle's eyes? Could she hold her own back?

"Thank you. Thank you for everything. I really didn't think you'd understand, but you do, don't you?"

"Yes. I do. Your father is not well, and I do fear that he will really hurt you someday. I've seen the signs. You have a good friend in Jim, and he is a smart man. He's thought this through, and I know that he'll take good care of you.... Go, now. I will keep your secret. Forever. I love you and will always hope for the best for you. Go." He made a small shooing gesture.

"Stay, Hobbs. Be a good dog." Now she could not hold back her tears. She wanted to say more, so much more. She looked longingly at her uncle. "Thank you. I love you, too."

And with that she was gone. Her journey had begun. Her journey to freedom, to safety, to Jim.

It was a long night. Peanut returned to her house and spent nearly an hour walking through every room, peering out every window, opening every cupboard door, drawer, and closet, re-living her fifteen years here—her home. She grabbed a duffel and filled it with what she could. She wouldn't need a lot—some clothes, a couple of pairs of shoes, a slicker, a book or two from her collection of favorites, the small amount of money she had stashed under the lamp by her bed. Seeing that there was still some room in the bag, she grabbed her blanket, the blanket her mother had made for her when she was born, the blanket she always bundled and held close to her heart as she slept. Leaving her room, she spotted the clam-shell necklace she had made the day before at Annie's birthday party—a keepsake from the beach, her home, a reminder of the infectious innocence and spirit of a seven-year-old girl, and, she hoped, a good luck charm to help guide her on this unknown journey. She hung it around her neck.

Darkness settled. It was time to leave. As promised, she climbed the tower stairs one last time to signal Jim that she was on her way. She carefully checked every inch of space in the tower and house to make sure she had left nothing behind that might lead her father to finding her. That is, if her father ever came home. Securing the house, she placed the key above the window shutter where those who knew would find it. She left everything in perfect order and with no sign of her disappearance.

Instead of taking the road past her uncle's farm, Peanut chose to walk the trail atop the rocky cliff at the edge of the shore. It was a dark night, and the winds were picking up. She could smell the sea. The air was damp, but at least it was warm. A summer storm was heading up the coast, but it was probably still an hour or so away. Enough time for her to get to the safety of the cottage.

She found Al's dory tied to a rock at the edge of the river. It was an hour or so after high tide, and the current was running out. She would have to row upstream, using all her strength to get across without being carried out to sea. She would secure the dory on the other side. Al would find it. He wouldn't know how it got there…or would he? Anyway, she would make sure it was safe.

Once across the river, she kept close to the water as she walked the half-mile beach. She could see lights in the cottages—summer residents and visitors hunkered down for what promised to be a stormy night. The smell of wood smoke from their cozy fires permeated the air and mixed with the salty spray of the sea. She would miss this. She would come back someday. Someday when it was safe.

Without the light of the moon and stars, Peanut carefully climbed the rock ledge at the south end of the beach up to the cottage. She had been in the cottage when Jim's family owned it, so she knew her way around. She let herself in the back kitchen door, which Jim had left unlocked for her. Once in, she bolted the lock and lit the small candle he had left in the pantry. She would not go upstairs or to the front of the house. She could not give any sign that she was there. A large upholstered chair sat in the corner of the dining room. She would settle there, taking her blanket from her bag, and wait.

END OF MAY 2017

*A*lthough somewhat disoriented and adjusting to life with a catheter, Dad has a few good days, and we both feel more comfortable with his new living situation. I use that time to be with Mom. She still eats some of her meals with assistance in the hallway, but she has her better days when she manages pretty well on her own and can join everyone else in the dining room. I am learning that with dementia there's no regular progression—in fact, there's nothing regular about it at all. You need to literally take one day, even a part of a day, at a time.

Today we sit at Mom's regular lunch table and are joined, once more, by Phyllis's daughter Nancy. She and I enjoy a lively conversation. Mom, Phyllis, Mary, and Anna, as do most of the residents, seem happiest when they have someone to listen to— not to be engaged themselves, but just to observe and listen, as they are today.

During my time around these aging men and women, I have become increasingly interested in their personal stories, each of which is unique and often fascinating if you are lucky enough to discover them. So I take advantage of this moment to ask Nancy about Phyllis.

"She'll be one hundred this fall," Nancy says proudly of her mother. "Pretty amazing. Her husband died sixteen years ago at the age of ninety-one; he was seven years older than her. That's when she moved here, at first to an independent living apartment, but more recently, we had to move her into the health center."

"Where did she live before coming here?"

"She and my dad spent most of their lives in Massachusetts, outside Boston. In 1990, they bought a cottage at Higgins Beach, and that's where they spent their summers before dad died. Mom still owns the cottage, so we go there occasionally—that is, when it's not rented out."

"So is that why she chose to come here?"

"Yes. She was actually one of the first residents."

"Sounds familiar. My parents moved here in 2005 and had an independent living apartment until just this year. Mom has been here in the health center almost two years, and we just moved Dad into assisted living. I guess we should count our blessings that we have these options right here in one place. I just can't imagine how it would be if they were still in Connecticut or in different facilities. It's hard enough dealing with all of this right here."

Oddly, it doesn't bother me to speak so frankly in the presence of Mom and her fellow residents. The cold truth has never had such a stark reality, and it is surprisingly easy to talk about.

"Does your mom like to talk about her life?" I ask as I look over at Phyllis and get a glimpse of a fleeting smile. "My mom has a lot of photographs so we look at those and enjoy remembering all the good times she's had. Right, Mom?" She's listening. Her head turns toward me with a nod.

"Actually, Mom has never talked much about her childhood," Nancy responds. "She has fond memories of marrying Dad, raising me and my two siblings, living what she always called a life she and Dad created out of hopes and dreams—in the way they wanted, with no one telling them what to do. They were very independent, I guess, and proud that they were able to bring goodness to others."

Placing her arm around Phyllis's shoulders, Nancy finishes with, "Yes, she had a good life, and it's wonderful to be able to continue to take her to the cottage where she can look out over the beach. It's a very special place for her. You should come with us sometime. It's the small shingled cottage on Cliff Street—the only one that hasn't been renovated or enlarged. It's original to its early 1900s construction."

"I'd love to. I walk that beach every day with my dog. I know exactly which cottage it is—it's actually my favorite because it's original. If I see you there I'll definitely stop by."

Pushing Mom back to her room, I turn out onto the deck for a breath of fresh air. The sun is out, and it's actually warm after a damp, gray, and cool May.

"Ahhh. Can we sit here for a bit? That sun feels good, doesn't it."

I park Mom in the shade of an umbrella, and she looks to the sky. It's nice to see her look up after spending most of her time slouched over with her eyes focused on the ground.

"Did you hear Nancy explain that Phyllis has a cottage at the beach?"

"Yes, the beach we walk."

"And the beach you went to for vacation with Bill and Janey when you turned seven. Remember? Your first visit to Maine. You had a special birthday party. You've been telling me a little bit about it."

"Yes. Pa said they were gone."

"Who, Mom? Some people at the beach?"

"He knew. He knew they were gone."

"Who was gone? Was this when you were there a long time ago?"

Mom starts to push her wheelchair, attempting to turn toward the door.

"Ready to go in? Back to your *zimmer*?"

I take over until she is through the doorway and facing straight ahead. With just a bit of guidance, she manages to push herself halfway down the hall toward her room before tiring out. Even though she doesn't think she knows where to go, she does.

"Can I go back to bed now?" Her safe space. Her place of peace.

"Of course, Mom. You've been up a long time. Time for a good nap."

Well, I'm having serious doubts about getting much more out of Mom about that first trip of hers to Maine, but, if nothing else, it is something to work her memory, something to get both our minds off her current condition and surroundings.

FRIDAY, JULY 22, 1932, PRE-DAWN

*S*unrise would come at 5:32 a.m. Jim hadn't slept. The inn was quiet. He was dressed, packed, ready to go. His pocket watch said 5:00. He placed his room key and a note on the bed: He was checking out a week early—his parents wanted him home for the last week of his vacation. Nothing wrong. Just some work for him to do for them on their house.

Peanut watched anxiously for a sign of life outside the darkened windows of the cottage. It had been a wild night with downpours of rain, thunder claps, crashing surf, an occasional bolt of lightning. The storm had passed quickly, though, as many do in the summer, and now it was quiet. Grabbing her bag, she waited in the kitchen doorway. Suddenly the low rumble of a car engine broke the silence.

The last piece of the plan that Jim had put in place the night before had gone well. Bill was right on time. Daylight had not yet broken. Jim appeared out of the darkness, Peanut stepped out of the cottage, and they both got into the car.

It was a painfully quiet fifteen-minute drive to the trolley stop, where Jim and Peanut got out to await the first run of the day to Portland. There they would catch the 8:00 train to Boston. Peanut stood holding her bag, head down, as Jim reached out to shake Bill's hand through the car window.

"Thank you, Mr. Walling. You've done us a great favor, and we appreciate your confidence and trust."

Bill nodded with a smile and pulled away. His early start at training for the CIA after his years in the army had served him well. He was back in his bed at the inn just as the first light of day broke over the horizon.

7:45 A.M.

"Did you hear that thunder last night?" Annie leaned off the side of her bed to face her sister.

"A little bit. Is it still raining?"

"A little bit! Boy, you sure are a good sleeper! I thought the sky was falling—you know that story? I thought it was really happening, and I saw flashes of light again out the window."

"Come on, Annie. Your imagination has no limits, does it? You must have gotten too much sun on the beach yesterday. Maybe today we should find something else to do."

"Not go to the beach? I want to explore those pools in the rocks some more. It was fun watching those little crabs swim around, and I collected thirty-eight periwinkles!"

"Good morning, dearies." Bill's gentle voice came through the doorway. "Looks like we had a storm last night, but it's a fine morning. Time to rise and shine!"

Sitting by the window having breakfast, the view was breathtaking. Everything glistened with drops of dew from the night's rain. It looked as if the world had been given a cleansing shower.

There was not a cloud in the sky. The ocean had calmed and looked more like a lake than the sea. Birds flew about gracefully, celebrating the passing of the storm. It was a new day. And upon reflection, Bill recognized its true significance. He smiled.

As high tide had taken most of the beach away this morning, Bill suggested a walk to The Pavilion to buy postcards for the girls to send to their mother. Writing letters, keeping in touch with family and friends, was an important life lesson Bill wanted to instill in his girls. A thank-you note to Jim and Peanut for the birthday party was also in order, but Bill knew better than to follow through with that. Maybe a note to the innkeepers for the delicious birthday cake would suffice.

The Pavilion was busy, mainly with clerks stocking the shelves in preparation for the weekend ahead.

"Pa, have we been here a whole week?" Annie looked around the store, amazed at all the activity. They had been rather secluded at the inn and on the beach, and she hadn't been to the store since her bike ride with Jim on their first full day of vacation.

"Yes. It's been a week—and there's one more to go, so don't start getting upset just yet.

"The postcards are over by the cash register. Why don't each of you pick two—one for your mother and one for your cousins in Cooperstown. And one for the innkeepers. I'll be over by the newspapers—haven't checked on what's going on in the world all week."

As Bill paused over the newspapers he couldn't help but overhear two men behind him.

"He left earlier in the week—not sure what day, but no one has seen him since. And he left that sweet daughter of his alone. I guess her uncle took her in. Don't know much more. He was bound to take off at some point. Just hasn't been himself since his wife died. I just feel sorry for the girl."

"Yeah, I heard he was rough on her. Poor kid. Good she has her uncle. Hey, gotta go. Let me know if you hear anything. See you at the market tomorrow?"

"Of course. Got the last of the strawberries this week. Maybe a bit of corn too—it's just about ready. Love that Silver Queen corn. See ya tomorrow."

Back at the inn, the girls diligently wrote their postcards, unedited by Bill and not terribly imaginative.

Dear Mother,

I'm fine. How are you? Having fun at the beach.

Love, Annie

Well, at least it was something, Bill mused. It's the thought that counts.

EARLY JUNE 2017

*I*t happens again only a week after our last trip to the emergency room, and this time I don't have to ask the nurse on the other end of the phone what's going on. The minute the phone rang and I saw the caller ID, I knew.

Same problem. Symptoms have worsened. Internal bleeding most likely due to Dad's annoyance with the catheter. He is released from the emergency room again at night, not as late as last time, but clearly prematurely. He's still bleeding!

The evening shift is on in assisted living, and they are not happy to see us return. We all know he was released too soon. An hour of chaos passes as they struggle to calm him down and deal with this literally bloody mess. He is miserable and I stand by, watching and knowing that this is not good. One nurse walks out declaring that her shift is over. At one point, I am left alone with him with absolutely no idea where everyone has gone and what is going to happen to Dad. He should go to the health center, and thankfully, later that night he does.

Three weeks. Three weeks with Mom and Dad just doors apart receiving the care they need. I admit I had thought I couldn't take any more of this—the month of May had been a total test of my inner strength—but here I am, and actually, everything seems quite under control. The health center staff are a true godsend.

It's nice to visit Mom now and be able to wheel her down the hall for a visit with Dad. We enter his room; he is in bed, eyes shut, relaxed.

"Hi, Dad. It's Kathy. I brought Mom to visit."

The joy I see in both of them fills Dad's room as he opens his eyes and gives the gift of his smile. What I am witnessing is so genuine and powerful. I am happy—for them and for myself. June 11th will be their sixty-ninth wedding anniversary. I can feel their everlasting love.

SATURDAY, JULY 23, 1932

The locals and beachgoers would call this the beginning of a "bad" week. The previous week had been a "good" week. The weeks alternated throughout the summer season—throughout the year, in fact—being determined by the tide. Annie learned this quickly as she pondered the view out the window this second Saturday morning of their vacation.

"Hey, Pa. Since we woke up, the ocean seems to be getting closer and closer—the beach is disappearing. That didn't happen last week."

"It's the tide, Annie. Remember I told you it goes from low to high and then high to low every six hours or so? It's changed a bit every day since we've been here. This past week, we had high tide in the mornings and evenings. When we were enjoying the beach in the middle of the day, it was low tide. But that has been changing. This week the low tide, the best beach time, will be early and late—there won't be much sand to play on in the middle of the day, and the tidal pools will be filled with water. Make sense?"

"Well, I guess so. But does that mean we can't go on the beach anymore?"

"Oh, no, no. Don't worry. Even at high tide, there's still a little beach to play on, just not as much—and sometimes the water comes all the way up to the seawall, so we won't be able to go down to the far end by the river for a couple of hours. There are plenty of other things we can do, though. I thought we might do a little exploring, like we did on Tuesday, in the roadster."

"Sounds good. I'm hungry." Close to but not quite a full-blown whine. "Is it time for breakfast?"

"It certainly is. I just need to shave and we'll go down."

Bill's daily shaving routine took about ten minutes that always seemed more like an hour to the girls. Patiently, Annie and Janey waited, gathering their postcards to mail and listening to the sounds of the inn coming alive.

"Hey, Janey, have you seen Jim? I don't think I've seen him since my birthday party, and that was three days ago. Can't hear his footsteps upstairs, either."

"Well, I don't exactly keep track of the other guests like you do, but no, I haven't seen him."

"Ready, dearies," Bill called through the doorway.

Breakfast was everyone's favorite meal.

Feeling like regulars now, Bill and the girls sat at what they considered "their" table, a nice table for four by the window. Annie was right, the tide was coming in, but after a midday excursion, they could come back to explore a whole new assortment of sea life on the beach.

"Pa, is our vacation already halfway over?" Annie inquired, looking a bit subdued.

"Yes, but we still have six full days of fun ahead. And with the tide as it is, I think we'll take the roadster and do some local exploring. I've been gathering a few ideas. We can enjoy the beach at the end of the day when the tide is low."

Annie sat pensively. This was her first real vacation, and it sure did seem to be going by fast. The first couple of days had gone slowly as they oriented themselves to their new surroundings, but after that, everything seemed to speed right by. Now it was the beginning of the end, and she wanted it all to just slow down. She didn't want it to end.

"Hello, Mr. Walling. Girls." The innkeeper approached in his typically welcoming fashion. "How is everyone this morning?"

"We were just thinking about a few road trips we might take in the next few days while we wait out the tide. Enjoy the beach later in the day."

"Good idea. If you need any suggestions, just let me know. There's plenty to see around here. And I imagine it would be fun in that car of yours."

"Top down! Hats on! Right, dearies? We'll have some fun exploring—maybe start off visiting Portland Head Light. I've heard it's the oldest lighthouse in Maine and very dramatic."

"Yes, it is, but before you head off, I did want to invite you to the inn's lobster bake on the beach tonight. We do this once a month in the summer for our guests and neighbors. Lobsters and all the fixings cooked right down in the sand! We gather anytime after six, usually eat around seven, and finish the night off with a bonfire."

"Oh, Pa! That sounds like fun! Can we go? Please? Hey, maybe Jim will be there." Annie looked up questioningly at the innkeeper.

"Actually, Jim checked out yesterday. A week early. He left a note that his folks needed him out in Michigan—they're fixing up their house and could use his help."

"I'm sorry we didn't get to say goodbye. He was a fine young man and very good to us," Bill responded.

"That he is. Anyway, can I count on you for the lobster bake?"

"Of course. We'd like nothing better. Sounds like fun—and delicious. Thank you."

It was only a twenty-minute drive to the lighthouse, and the views there were beautiful. Bill was able to explain the history of the lighthouse, as he had done some reading about it at the inn. It had stood here for almost a century and a half. The girls looked up in awe, imagining the sixteen oil lamps shining brightly while the lighthouse keeper kept an eye out for British ships. There were no ships today, just a lobster boat or two and an expanse of ocean as far as the eye could see.

There were nearly thirty people at the lobster bake that evening, and Annie and Janey quickly joined a group of children gathering seaweed for the fire. The men had dug a large hole and filled it with layers of seaweed, lobsters, corn, and clams. On the bottom was a bed of coals and the seaweed trapped in the heat and moisture. Mother Nature's oven.

It was a messy and unforgettable feast topped off with freshly baked blueberry cake. Stuffed and stretched out on blankets, Annie and Janey watched the southwestern sky explode into a medley of colors as the sun began to set. Dramatic clouds swirled above, changing from red to orange to purple as the sun's rays played on the horizon.

"It's a good one," the innkeeper said to Bill as they joined the cleanup crew. "We get some spectacular sunsets here, and this one sure doesn't disappoint."

"Yes, you certainly have it all right here in this tiny corner of the world. I'm so glad I decided to bring the girls here—they're having a great time. And we've especially enjoyed the friendship of the local people. Annie's birthday party over at Peanut's house, thanks to Jim and Peanut, was far beyond my expectations. And thank you for the cake."

"Jim's a great guy. He's always had his eyes out for Peanut, being an only child and all. She's a nice girl. Don't see much of her when Jim's not around, and now he's had to head on his way. Glad you got to know them a bit."

The bonfire was lit just as the sun set, and Bill curled up with his girls, each with her head resting on his knee, eyes glued to the night sky. Six more days. Not knowing when he would be with them next—probably not until Christmas—Bill sank into the comfort of their presence, their innocence, their love, and counted his blessings.

MID- TO LATE JUNE 2017

*A*n increasingly familiar feeling overcomes me. I don't know if I can make a difference anymore. She's farther gone now than ever before, and this time, it doesn't seem as if she will rally back. My son and his family are coming this weekend. Maybe she'll be better, maybe not.

I have what will be my last lunch with Mom. I find her at one of the tables where the nurses are feeding the residents. This is a first—and not good. Jessica leans over, placing a spoonful of something soft and mushy against Mom's lips. Nothing. I try, also with no success, but do hear her whisper, "No, thank you." She will forever be the good girl she lived her life to be.

June 10th. My son, his wife, and my two- and four-year-old grandchildren pay a visit. Mom is now in a Broda chair, a wheelchair that reclines, is heavily cushioned, and has an extended footrest and high sides to provide extra support. The nurses have her in the hallway where they can keep an eye on her. She is asleep, her head resting on an old keepsake pillow of hers, the one with a photograph printed on it—a photo of her and my brother donning souvenir hats and T-shirts when the New York Rangers won the Stanley Cup. I take her picture; it's the last picture I will ever take of her. My granddaughter goes over and gives her a gentle kiss. My grandson approaches her and waves. My son and daughter-in-law look on with a mix of love, sadness, pride—a jumble of emotions that will never be forgotten. I know because I seem to live with the same ones every day now.

Mom sleeps during my visits. I am told that she is eating a bit, but at our family meeting with the nurses and staff we are asked if we would consider Hospice. You know, I think, those people who come and sit by the side of the dying and pray for them. Wrong. It's so much more.

We agree to sign up, and the next day I meet with a representative to review their services and sign the paperwork. They begin their work almost immediately, assigning nurses, a social worker, and a member of the clergy (with our approval), and their daily attention ensues. If I am not there during their comings and goings, my phone rings each evening with an update.

June 22. Mom is getting the medical, physical, emotional, and spiritual attention she needs and deserves. Dad is still down the hall, and Hospice is there to provide moral support for him, as well. I doubt he says much during their visits, but I do know that he benefits from their presence. I certainly do. For a time, I no longer feel so alone.

June 26. Dad's healthy enough to return to assisted living. Maybe he'll actually get to settle in this time and enjoy his new apartment. My sister spends three nights at my house, and her company lightens the air. We read about dying in the materials from Hospice. (Do you know what "active dying" is? We didn't.) We pull out my photos of our trip together to Europe in 1976 and laugh. We eat well. We visit Mom and read her prayers from *Small Rain*, a keepsake of mine given to me by my godparents on my first birthday. We spend time with Dad. We walk on the beach with my dog. Everything is, for now, quite stable.

June 29. My sister leaves.

June 30. It's Friday, not that that matters. I think I'll enjoy a quiet day for myself. The sun is out, and I take my book and my dog outside to soak it all in and put the cares of the world aside. I can feel and smell the sea breeze. The birds are playfully passing from shrub to tree sharing in the joy of spring. The garden is a blaze of yellow with evening primrose in full bloom. A touch of humidity hangs in the air, left from the morning fog. Sigh…the deep breath that emerges involuntarily when I am completely relaxed.

Sunday, July 24–Friday, July 29, 1932

*T*ime flew by, as the last few days of vacations typically do. A rainy Sunday kept Bill, Janey, and Annie at the inn entertaining themselves playing backgammon, picking up books that had sat unattended for a few days, and welcoming long afternoon naps. Summer rain had its way of slowing everything down. At first, it created some frustration for the girls, but once they discovered the cozy fire, blankets, and throw pillows in the inn's sitting room, they melted into the warm comfort of their surroundings.

Monday, Tuesday, Wednesday. Blue skies returned, Bill lowered the top on the roadster, and off they went. Being the pilot that he was, Bill insisted they visit the nearby Portland Airport. He had only heard about it because, five years earlier, Charles Lindbergh had attempted to land there. Unfortunately, his plane had been diverted due to fog and ended up on a beach farther south.

Tuesday's adventure took them to the famous arcade and pier five miles south at Old Orchard Beach. After a long walk on the seven-mile beach, Bill parked himself on a bench while the girls tried out the carousel (apparently the very first in the United States) and Noah's Ark funhouse. They ended their adventure gazing at the expanse of ocean, so much more exposed than at Higgins Beach, from the end of what had been the world's longest steel pier when it was built in 1898.

"It's amazing that all the way up here there's such a famous place, Pa," Annie reflected as Bill told her of the many distinctions held by Old Orchard Beach. "You'd think all the biggest, the best, the firsts would be in a place like New York."

They stayed closer to home on Wednesday. Now high tide wasn't until early afternoon, so the morning was spent on the beach. As a special treat after lunch, Bill drove them up the road to Len Libby Candies, a family-owned candy-making company known particularly for its delicious chocolates. The girls filled their bags to the brim, Bill's more structured rules having become quite relaxed at this point in their vacation.

Annie looked questioningly at Bill over dinner that night.

"Hey, Pa, do you think we could go to the farm tomorrow? It's our last day, and I want to see Rhubarb again. Maybe Peanut will be there and we can say goodbye."

"That should be OK. Why don't we enjoy one last morning on the beach and then go over and see who's around after lunch? Janey? Is that all right with you?"

All evening and the following morning, Bill could not stop debating with himself whether or going to the farm was a good idea. Of course, Peanut would not be there—but was he the only one who knew that? To play it safe, he would have to assume so. He wasn't one to lie—he would not lie. He would just have to be very careful and hope they had a brief, cordial visit. No questions asked.

The farm was bustling when they arrived, and they found Peanut's uncle out in the fenced pasture with three of the horses. One was Rhubarb.

"Rhubarb!" An observer would have thought Annie owned the horse!

"Oh, hi, Annie," Peanut's uncle warmly greeted her as she ran toward him and the horses. "Nice to see you again. How have you been since your party?"

"We've been soooo busy! We leave tomorrow. I had to see Rhubarb one more time." Annie reached out to rub the horse's soft muzzle.

"Here, give him this apple. He'll love you even more for it."

Feeding Rhubarb the apple, Annie looked around. "Is Peanut here? We wanted to say goodbye. Has her father come home yet?"

"Actually, no and yes."

Annie listened with a puzzled look on her face.

"Her father did come home a couple of days ago, but Peanut was invited to one of her friend's lake houses for a couple of weeks, so she's not here. She left the day after your party. Won't be back for another week at least."

"Oh, that's too bad. See—I'm wearing the necklace she showed me how to make at the party! It's my souvenir from vacation. It will always make me happy."

"Glad you have it to remember us by and this special place we call home. I do hope you'll come back someday."

"You can bet I will!" Annie shouted back as she ran to her father, who was waiting with Janey by the car.

Bill was relieved that Annie had taken care of business on her own and that he hadn't had to speak to anyone.

"Let's go, girls. One last stop at The Pavilion, and then we should head back and pack a little. We have a long drive tomorrow and will have to leave right after breakfast."

"Can we take one last walk on the beach before we leave, Pa?"

"If you're up early and ready to go, of course we can, Annie dear."

FRIDAY, JUNE 30, 2017

I hear the phone inside, someone leaving a message. I guess I better check.

Caller ID—the health center. Message: I think you better come over. Time: 1:18 p.m.

4:20 p.m. She's gone. Her obituary will read "died peacefully with family at her side." Isn't that what they all say? Yes, in the end she was at peace. Yes, a few minutes before she passed, she let go of the grip she'd had on the bedrail for weeks. Yes, family was at her side, actually enjoying a "picnic" of egg salad sandwiches, chips, and cookies provided by the health center (when they bring food, you know the time has come).

My reflection on those three hours will forever be imprinted with every minute detail in my heart and soul. I did open the window—not realizing at the time that you're supposed to do that to let the spirit out. I did get Dad from the apartment, and he sat close by her head where, if she opened her eyes, she could see him. I did acknowledge the nurse as she told me she was going to give her a bit more morphine. I did stand up to throw away my paper plate and, looking down, realized she had stopped breathing. I did say thank you to her when it was finally over. And I did give her one last kiss.

I look over at Dad who is clearly enjoying his sandwich. "Dad." No response. "Dad. She's gone."

"Oh? Really?" He is very calm.

"I guess we should go back up to the apartment."

"OK."

The world seems so incredibly still. Almost empty of any stimulation. I discover that the assisted living staff have not been told anything. They have no idea that my father has just lost the love of his life—that I have lost my mother. A fury builds within me, but I know that won't help anything. Wait. Calm down. Why should they know? It's only been thirty minutes.

I need to get Dad into his chair. He will nap. I need to tell everyone around what has happened. Then I will go home, my dog at my side, knowing there's nothing else I can do.

Sunday, July 2, 2017

*S*unday brunch. Isn't that what we've done every week for the past twelve years? I can't break the routine now. It's especially important for Dad, who looks forward to this time to be among the familiar faces of the retirement community in the attractive and comfortable main dining room. And maybe it's important for me, too, a bit of normalcy for us both. Dad and I have had brunch alone for the past two years since Mom has been in the health center, so it won't be that different. Hopefully, as nice as they are, the people around us will respect our privacy and not shower us with condolences.

I arrive just before 11 a.m. Dad is up, dressed, in his chair—clearly he knows it's Sunday, time for brunch. He seems fine, but it has always been a challenge to "read" him because his quiet, reserved nature dominates, and he's very good at burying his emotions.

"Hey, Dad. In the mood for brunch today?"

"What time is it?"

"Oh, a little after eleven."

"We go at eleven thirty, right?"

"Yes, that's when we usually go, but we can go now if you're hungry. Let me just make your bed and then we can go."

Leaving my barking dog (who I've timed and who will typically relax after three or four minutes), we head down the hall. Dad is now using Mom's walker, and although at a pace that would try anyone's patience, he gets where he needs to go.

"Shall we cross over the walkway, or would you like to go down and cross over outside—get a little fresh air?"

"Do we have time for some fresh air?" Dad has always been very conscious of being on schedule.

"Oh, sure. We're early."

Exiting the elevator on the ground floor, we run into Phyllis and Nancy also heading out.

"So sorry to hear about your mom," Nancy gives me a tender hug.

"Thank you." What else can you really say? "You headed out?"

"We're taking Phyllis to the beach cottage for lunch. Such a perfect summer day."

"Sounds nice." I lean over to face Phyllis and greet her with a smile. "How are you today, Phyllis?"

Smile. Eyes twinkling. A soft, "Just fine, thank you," surprises me; Phyllis has never said very much, at least when I'm around.

"Have a nice time at the beach. OK?"

A mumbled "OK" is accompanied by another smile as Phyllis pushes her walker toward the car.

I have to ask Nancy a question. Dad seems eager to shuffle on, so I let him go, knowing I can very easily catch up.

"Hey, Nancy. I noticed your mom is wearing a shell necklace. It looks homemade." And I think to myself that it actually it looks a bit familiar.

"Oh, that," Nancy says, breaking a laugh. "She's had that *forever*! She wears it whenever we go to the beach cottage. She says she made it when she was a teenager, and that it brings her good luck." Another chuckle. "I'm surprised she hasn't broken or lost it by now. Funny the things I am learning about her these days."

"Yeah, I've learned a lot about my mom and dad, too. It's amazing. I guess it takes getting to this stage to realize how much you don't know."

And I ponder how much you can discover if only you take the time to be there, to listen, to look, to learn. I will forever be grateful for the precious time I've shared with Mom and Dad these past few months, years. A blessing that I never planned on, looked for, even asked for—a blessing that was, I guess, just meant to be.

"Well, we must go. Have a nice brunch." Nancy steps into the car after securing Phyllis's seat belt for her.

"Thanks. Enjoy your time at the cottage. One of these days, I do want to come by and see it."

Epilogue

*D*ad lived another nine months. In that time, he fell and fractured his hip, battled chronic urinary tract infections, and spent the last seven of those months in the health center—room 203 (Mom had been in room 214 down the same "Higgins Beach" hallway). I had actually not been in the health center for all of seven weeks (wow!), but here we were again—me, my dog, and now my father.

Fortunately, Dad had the same nurses who had taken care of Mom, so there were literally no surprises and actually many pleasant moments with my "second family." Jessica (who, to Dad, became Erika), Sarah, Mike, Erwin, Joanne, Donna, Arthur, Bobbie, Sandy, Alis, Mariah, Lisa, Ralph.... The list goes on—caring, friendly, and familiar people I will never forget.

Mom "visited" me and Dad regularly, leaving valentine sand dollars and geranium blossoms, sending butterflies and birds our way, making sure the sixty-foot tree that fell behind my house one snowy March night did not crush my bedroom and me, and assuring Dad that she was doing just fine in her cute little white house with its gardens.

I talked to Dad a lot, asking a lot of questions, realizing that there was so much I had never learned from my mother. We had fun with his childhood memories, my research into the jewelry company his great-grandfather and grandfather had owned, his genealogy, and reading his "Life Story (so far)" that he had written by hand after his retirement in 1990. Every day began with him recalling his crazy dreams, fortunately laughing, as his mind revisited the places of his past. They only turned concerning for me once, the night he dreamt, multiple times, that Mom had come back with her "new husband."

"What is she doing having so much fun, leaving me to endure this?"

Those were his exact words, and I knew at that moment that he had made up his mind.

Dad passed "peacefully with family at his side" on March 25, 2018. The window was open. Forty minutes before his death, he said his last word, *"STAY,"* as my son and I were about to leave the room for a minute. We stayed.

Phyllis is alive and well and will hopefully enjoy more summer afternoons on the porch of her Higgins Beach cottage. I retrieved Mom's shell necklace from the Do Not Throw Away box and will cherish it forever.

Very few people remain who lived at Higgins Beach in the 1930s. No one seems to remember anything about the young man named Jim and the girl named Peanut from across the river. The Breakers Inn continues to enjoy a thriving summer business. I walk the beach daily with my dog and reflect on all that I have to be thankful for—in large part due to my mother and father.

There are the 62 photo albums. There is the furniture, clothing, paintings, jewelry…all my parents' lifelong possessions left behind for their children and grandchildren to adopt as their own. But for me, nothing will ever come close to the value of the enduring love, friendship, and trust I received from both my mother and my father in the final years of their lives. That is what I carry with me as I continue my chosen path.

Janey and Annie, 1932

The Breakers Inn
Photo courtesy of Rodney Laughton

AUTHOR'S NOTE

*M*y first thought of writing a book came during my regular walks on Higgins Beach a number of years ago after visits with my parents at the retirement community, typically on Sundays for brunch. When I moved to the area two years ago, and my walks on the beach became daily, the idea of a book grew. I always walk slowly on the beach, taking in all of nature's splendor, which changes daily, if not hourly. On this beach, however, I found myself also looking off to a point of land to the east with a picturesque and distinctive house perched on the rocky ledge surrounded by trees and fields. *A murder could have happened out there*—the thought of a mind seeking distraction from the realities of life. *Someday I will write a mystery novel about that house.*

It was Sunday, May 28, 2017, that the book—or should I say, *writing* the book—became my salvation, and it would be so for nearly a year. It turned out that I couldn't write a murder—it's not in my nature—so it became a mystery, and a very simple one at that. It also became a personal memoir of sorts as I stood by my parents during the last few months of their lives.

That Sunday, I woke up feeling overwhelmed by the challenges of a dying mother, an increasingly dependent father and his move to assisted living, the dispersal of my parents' belongings, and the constant unpredictable situations that stopped me in my tracks. I needed a reset button—you know, like those red buttons on the backs of computers or TVs that you push and voilá! it works! I started to write.

The book evolved in parallel with everything around me. I found pleasure, and solace, in the writing, but even more so in digging into my past, my parents' past, and the past of this little beach community in my backyard that I love. It became, in a fashion, a tapestry of moments and emotions woven into a simple story of love and trust.

I would like to thank Rodney Laughton for sharing his knowledge of local history and The Breakers Inn. Gratitude goes out to my dog-walking beach friends and the nursing home staff for their ongoing encouragement, friendship, and support. The enthusiasm I received from Phyllis and her family, and the tour of their Higgins Beach cottage was inspirational. I spent hours over my mother's photo albums and letters to her from her father from WWI and WWII. Thanks to the internet, I was able to jump in and out of research about little bits of my family history, Morse code, tide/sunrise/sunset data, histories of the railroad and trolley industries, old photos of the area, 1900s house construction, local businesses, and other little details as I strove to keep the book historically accurate. In the end, however, my greatest inspiration and source for this story was my heart and the experiences I had on a journey that I never imagined I would take.